The "C" Students Guide to Scholarships

A Creative Guide to Finding Scholarships When Your Grades Suck and Your Parents are Broke!

Felecia Hatcher

About Peterson's Publishing

To succeed on your lifelong educational journey, you will need accurate, dependable, and practical tools and resources. That is why Peterson's is everywhere education happens. Because whenever and however you need education content delivered, you can rely on Peterson's to provide the information, know-how, and guidance to help you reach your goals. Tools to match the right students with the right school. It's here. Personalized resources and expert guidance. It's here. Comprehensive and dependable education content—delivered whenever and however you need it. It's all here.

For more information, contact Peterson's, 2000 Lenox Drive, cqx, Lawrenceville, NJ 08648; 800-338-3282 Ext. 54229; or find us online at www.petersonspublishing.com.

Bernadette Webster, Managing Editor; Editor; Ray Golaszewski, Publishing Operations Manager

ISBN-13: 978-0-7689-3615-5
ISBN-10: 0-7689-3615-2

Printed in the United States of America

10 9 8 7 6 5 4 3 2 1   14 13 12

Dedication

I dedicate this book to my high school guidance counselor who told me that I could not make it to college because of my GPA and to "C" students everywhere who have been told by others that they could not achieve greatness and used that comment as motivation to prove them wrong.

Table of Contents

Table of Contents

Table of Contents

Foreword

If a college graduate told you she paid for her education with $100,000 in scholarship money even though her high school grade point average (GPA) was less than 3.0 would you believe her? If you had a student preparing for college wouldn't you be the least bit curious to hear her story? That's what this book is all about.

I was excited to write the foreword to this book because as a father of four children with a 16-year-old getting ready for college, I needed a practical guide to help navigate the daunting and somewhat complicated waters of finding money for college. With college tuition on the rise, I understand the possibility of not being able to afford college. This book could not have come at a better time.

When I first met Felecia many years ago, she asked me to speak to her student group at her college. I was impressed by her professionalism and by the fact that she was running a nonprofit called Urban Excellence at such a young age. She explained to me that she helped students find money for college. So, I asked the next logical question, "What makes you qualified to do that?" She simply told me that she had won $100,000 in scholarships and wanted to help others do the same.

Being told that she should not look into college because of her grades didn't crush her dreams; it only made her work that much harder. In her book she shows you do not have to be defined by a GPA and she shares exactly what she did to win those scholarships. Unlike other cold, research-compiled books on finding money for college, Felecia provides motivational as well as the impactful wisdom and techniques that are needed for students and parents to successfully win money for college. Felecia may have been a "C" student in high school but she is not a "C" student in life, and she will show you how to take charge of your destiny.

I am also excited to have had the privilege over the years of watching Felecia become tremendously successful in business. As one of the top rising entrepreneurs under 30 in the country, she still has the desire of that 19-year-old college student who wanted to empower other students. So, whether you're a "C" student or an "A" student, a broke parent or a parent who can afford to pay for college, you need to pay attention to the pages in this book. Through her experience, Felecia has become my *College Financial Coach*, and with three more children to send to college, I am so thankful for her guidance.

Nathan E. Burrell Founder/CEO

Helping Our Nations Empowering Youth Project

Preface

This book is as much about uncovering scholarships as it is about personal marketability; your grades may not be your strongest point but I am going to help you find out what is. You are not a walking GPA. You are an individual with unique talents. Someone wants to give you a chance; all you need are the tools to put your best foot forward. I wrote this book because I've run into thousands of kids who've had horrible teachers and guidance counselors who have shattered their dreams of going to college by telling them that their grades define them and define their lives. Yes grades are important, but if you have had mishaps like I did when I was in high school, you still deserve to go to college and you deserve a chance to be a ROCKSTAR! So I wrote this book to empower you and your parents to say "Screw the people that won't help me with my future! I'm going to do it myself!"

Remember this: "C" students are:

COOL, CREATIVE, & COURAGIOUS
and deserve to get
CASH for COLLEGE!

Introduction
This Book is For You, Slacker!

Your Grades Suck...
But You Still Want to Go to College, Right?

Many people have asked me, "Why is your book called *The "C" Students Guide to Scholarships?*" Well, I've looked around, and I've noticed there are way too many scholarship resources out there geared toward brainiacs. If you academic slackers don't know any better (and many of you don't, because you haven't slowed down long enough to ask), you might think that only National Honor Society students with a 4.0 GPA have a glimmer of a chance to score big scholarship money for college—not-so-brilliant, yet happy and well-adjusted students need not apply.

This stereotype is simply NOT TRUE! I was an average student in high school, with a GPA that fluctuated between 2.1 and 2.7, and I still succeeded in paying my way through college with scholarships and grant awards. I got fed that same line you've probably heard time and again: "If you don't pull those grades up, you can forget about a university degree. You'll be doomed to spend your days at a community college and your nights flipping burger patties at McDonalds!" I took the words of these naysayers to heart, and I tried my very hardest to raise my GPA to a 3.0—the bare minimum everyone told me I had to maintain if I didn't want to hear the scholarship committee members laugh in my face, but it just wasn't happening for me. It seemed that every time I started to crack a book, the phone would ring and one of my friends would start telling me something that was SO much more interesting than analyzing the events leading up to the War of 1812.

Lucky for you (and, of course, for me), I walked away from the people telling me I could never win a scholarship with my fists clenched and my mind screaming, "Screw them!" Being a "C" student doesn't mean that you are dumb, and it doesn't mean that you can't succeed in life. It means that you are a creative student, a cool student, and that you are complicated and courageous. Sure your grades suck and your parents are broke, but don't use those minor obstacles as an excuse to not pursue your dreams. My story makes me an ambassador of hope for those out there who are not quite "college material," but choose to reject such a life-crippling label. I'm living proof that "C" students can find scholarship success! If *I* could win $120,000 in free money for college, then so can you! The trick is digging a little bit deeper and asking yourself, "Why can't I go to college?" If your grades aren't your strongest asset, then you'll have to find other ways to market yourself to scholarship committees. There are many scholarships out there that don't require—or even expect—applicants to have a stellar academic record. Between the outrageous Duck Tape scholarships, the sports scholarships for bench-warmers, and even the (*you've gotta' be kidding me*) write-an-essay-about-bees types of scholarships, you are sure to find *something* that will compliment your personal strengths and put money right into your pocket!

This book is for all "C" students, my friends, kindred spirits—those who may have encountered a few bumps along their scholastic road or who may have found their television production class far more entertaining than their geometry class—who are well-rounded and each special in their own way. All the years I spent searching for college scholarship money, I never found a book that spoke to *me*—the ambitious "C" student. I hope this book will speak to YOU! I hope it will motivate you to show all those brainiacs at your high school that you can win just as many college scholarships as they do!

Why "C" Students Rock!

Every kid begins day one of freshman year with a 4.0 GPA. For some of us, it's all downhill from there. Education is a beautiful thing, but equating the volume of a sphere or conjugating French verbs can only hold a creative person's interest for so long. In my teenaged mind, there were so many components to school that were way more interesting than what was being taught in the classroom, for example, basketball, boys, my friends, boys, creative writing for fun, and, did I mention, boys?

At the mid-point of my freshman year, my GPA had dwindled down to a 2.125. I remember the exact number, because it just happened to be the last four digits of our home phone number. Mostly thanks to my disdain for math, I couldn't manage to pull my grade up to a 3.0 by my senior year.

Of course, the day eventually came for that inevitable trip to discuss my future with my school guidance counselor. I told the woman about my top five dream schools, I then sat back waiting for her words of confidence and encouragement. My advisor looked at me with a serious expression on her face and said, "Felecia, your grades are horrible. You won't ever attend a university. You should focus instead on finding a vocational school or getting a trade."

I was devastated! *This* was the woman who the school board had hired to steer their students down the correct path in life and, most importantly, to motivate them? After throwing a few mental darts at my guidance counselor's face, I resolved that I would be accepted into a great college even without her help. Maybe *she* couldn't see past my poor grades to the resourceful person I am underneath, but I knew the truth about myself and other "C" students!

My GPA-obsessed counselor overlooked the "real world" smarts that a person develops when he or she is trying to juggle life's obligations and pleasures, but these are the type of skills that can prove very useful for future college students. For example, I always made sure that my quarterly schedule included one or two "easy" classes—non-demanding periods that I could use to begin (and sometimes even finish!) my homework. This tactic freed up time after school for volunteer work and social activities. Another favorite school survival trick of mine was to always carry a recording device in my backpack. If I ever *really* didn't want to pay attention to the teacher or *really* didn't feel like taking notes, I could click on my recorder and lean back for a nap. The material was then available for me to review whenever I felt more alert and focused, without scrambling to copy a friend's notes at the last minute. If you can relate to my per:

high school experience, then I know you're a bona fide "C" student, 'cause that's how we operate!

So, yes, I was a "C" student, and I am totally proud of it! Being laz…err, having a different set of priorities than those 4.0-bookworm-types can open up a whole new world of opportunities for uniqueness and creativity.

Straight-A students may possess the study skills and focus that we lack, but straight-C students are more adaptable to unexpected change and more resourceful when it comes time to find solutions to problems. Kids who always have their homework prepared and ready to turn in on time, miss out on the challenge of thinking up bizarre reasons why they should be allowed to hand in their assignments late…a creative process that helps "C" students think of new angles for presenting themselves to scholarship committees!

Has someone ever said, you could have finished your homework *twice* in the time it took you to plot out an excuse for why you should do it later? Yes, that's us! "C" students have hidden talents for using McGyverish (and sometimes McGooberish) tactics to find the most resourceful way of getting around our problems, even the ones we've created for ourselves! These talents may not be the type that can catapult us to the top of the school Honor Roll list, but they will serve us well out in the "real world," where life is not so scheduled and predictable.

There are plenty of A-students who can handle both their schoolwork and extracurricular activities, but I've also seen many of my peers crash and burn when they try to take on too much. As "C" students, we are never at risk of making ourselves sick because we're trying to succeed in multiple facets of life. We decide what's most important to us—the activities that we enjoy the most—and we accept that our schoolwork is going to come in second place when we are choosing how to spend our day. While our GPAs may suffer for it, "C" students are often well-rounded and happier people overall. Lucky for us, these *other*, less-academic talents can win us scholarships as easily as high grades can…if we set our minds to making it happen.

Mission Impossible—
2.1 GPA to $100,000 for College:

My Scholarship Story

I was born into a family that values education and hard work. But growing up was not easy. My parents both deferred pursuing college degrees until my brother and I were teenagers. So throughout middle school and most of high school, we were all in school. Through sheer determination, my parents have now achieved their personal life goals against all odds. My father who left rural Georgia on his own at the age of 16, now owns a top construction development company and my mom, an immigrant from Jamaica, also blazed her own path to a Ph.D. and a successful career as an educator.

My parents really struggled to provide for my brother* and me when we were kids. We had big shoes to fill if we expected to live up to such strong examples of dedication and success, but little bro and I didn't even bother to try. We were too busy enjoying the fun things in life, like sports, television, and friends, to pay much attention to boring ol' school. Our mom couldn't understand how she had raised two total slackers, and one day she decided to do something about it. She sat us kids down and delivered an ultimatum:

"I love you both, but if you two lazy brats want to continue living in this house, I need to see you either planning for college or preparing to join the military."

The military was not an option for me! I'd rather sit through a thousand college lectures than get up at 5 a.m. even ONE morning to do push-ups and jumping jacks. It was time to start seriously planning out my higher education…but how would I ever pay for *that*?

I've told you about my parents' successful careers, of course, but they were working class people with debts and expenses of their own. There was no 529-college savings plan or million dollar trust fund waiting around to be spent on my college tuition. My parents would have loved to write me a big check and shove me in the direction of a university, but they weren't financially able to foot my education bill at that time. Even now, I doubt they could manage it—college is freakin' expensive!

Winning scholarships was the first idea that popped into my head after I'd made my decision to tackle the challenge of paying my own way through college, but I was scared that my dismal grades would gum up the works enough to bring that dream to a grinding halt. I tried to raise my GPA, of course, but decided that my energy would be better spent on rounding out my extracurricular activities. I began paying less attention to basketball and started joining more clubs. As a consequence, my court performance suffered and I saw less and less game time. Any dreams I had of playing professional ball for the WNBA were benched right along with me.

No worries, because I had a secret plan. The summer between my junior and senior years of high school, I got an awesome job working for a business that would guarantee my future success…yep, McDonald's! Think about it. Have you ever heard a story about a poor person turned billionaire that didn't begin with him or her working at McDonald's?

But I couldn't put all my faith in flipping Big Macs, so as my senior year began, I continued to dabble in different activities that would make me a well-rounded person. I was feeling very mature as I took charge of my own education, and I knew it was time to actually begin applying for those scholarships!

Wednesday was scholarship day at my high school. Our not-so-helpful guidance counselor would lay out all available scholarship applications on a table and leave them there for anyone who bothered to drop by to take a look. When I finally got up the courage to check and see if it was really true that there were scholarships for people who could write well, but had poor grades, I was disappointed by the paltry selection. I have to attribute much of my eventual success to Miss Fontaine, our amazing

career counselor. She explained the scholarship process in a really down-to-earth way, and encouraged me not to give up. "Come back and check as often as you can," she said, "and you'll be sure to find something."

The scholarship applications were only left out for 30 minutes each week, so I decided that my best strategy was to pick up every application. I took them home with me, and every Wednesday night I would read them over to see if I qualified to apply. If I didn't qualify, *could* I qualify? Did I need more community service? Could I join a certain club, or get a job with a certain company? What if I dug deeper into my parents' background? This became my process of elimination. Usually I could use public relations tactics to spin the scholarships into my favor, but if that didn't work, the application would be added to the "Maybe Later" pile.

As I worked out a system for filling out my scholarship paperwork, I began to really enjoy the process. It was almost like an adrenaline rush to get an application completed and sent off. But I began to get discouraged, because I knew that the next step in the game was getting a phone call from someone who would say, "Congratulations! You are the winner!" Or maybe they would just show up at my house with balloons and one of those over-sized checks? I was waiting for that day...but it never came. Well, at least not until November, when I finally received that phone call that I been anticipating for what seemed like my whole life!

Sadly, my first call to interview as a scholarship finalist ended in defeat and disappointment. In early January, I got a letter that was *supposed* to be my late Christmas present. But, instead of post-yuletide cheer, the envelope contained my first scholarship rejection letter. That was bad but then it got worse. Shortly after, I received not one, but TWO rejection letters from colleges on my "Dream List." I felt so bummed out and disheartened that I actually signed up to take the ASVAB, which is a competency test for people who are military-bound. I was seriously entertaining the idea of joining the Marines, even though it took all my strength and will power just to walk into their recruitment office. I figured I could put in a few years of service and retire with the pockets of my fatigues filled with money for college. I had pretty much given up on actually winning a scholarship, but with my Scholarship Express Package system in place, sending out applications was too easy to stop all together.

My luck (based on my skill, of course!) turned around the next two months, and I went out on at least five more interviews. And I started winning the scholarships! They were all small monetary amounts, like the $300 one from my dad's fraternity, Phi Beta Sigma. By the end of March, I'd collected $2,000 worth of small scholarships. It was a tidy sum, of course, but hardly enough to pay for my freshman-year books!

Then along came Senior Awards Night—a ceremony that totally changed my life. Students and parents sat together in the school auditorium, listening to names being announced and applauding politely as the "smart" kids accepted huge checks. I was probably the only "C" student who was sitting on the edge of her seat in anticipation. I had applied for many of the scholarships that were being awarded, but as the evening wound to its close, I had yet to hear my own name blare out through the scratchy sound system. The presenters seemed to announce each winner in slow motion, as if they were intentionally toying with me. My anxiety level mounted with each passing minute.

I'd pretty much lost all hope by the time three familiar-looking old ladies took the stage. They were representatives from the League of Women Voters, with whom I had interviewed for a small scholarship. I felt newly-formed ulcers gnawing at the lining of my stomach; I just couldn't take any more disappoint. I looked away from the stage as if I just didn't care, and I was even tempted to plug my ears. It's a good thing that I didn't, because one of the women stepped up to the mic and announced:

"This scholarship goes to an outstanding young girl ... Felecia Hatcher!"

What? Who? Me? REALLY???

It was finally my turn to take the stage and beam at the jealous onlookers as cameras nearly blinded me with flashing clicks. The presentation of my award was a bittersweet moment because the person who handed me the giant check was none other than the very same guidance counselor who had told me I was only fit to attend a trade school. I wished I could give her a nice shove—possibly off the side of the stage—and say, "I don't want you in this picture, lady! The only way you helped me get to where I am now was by giving me the motivation to prove you wrong!" As I left the stage, it took all of my willpower not to slap my butt and shout to my guidance counselor that she could kiss it.

After my first scholarship acceptance, I was suddenly bouncing back and forth from that stage like a yo-yo. I barely had time to settle back down in my seat before my name was called again…and again…and again. These were all relatively small scholarships, but needless to say my confidence had swelled to mammoth proportions by the time someone stepped up to announce the winners of the Community and Schools Scholarship. This was the big one! Four FULL RIDES were being handed out to attend colleges in the surrounding Florida area. I glanced nervously across the room at my friend, Patrick. Since my winning streak had begun, he and I were running neck-to-neck as the school's top contenders for collecting scholarship dollars. We both desperately wanted the free ride to Lynn University. And then…Patrick's name was called.

… But not for the coveted LU prize.

Patrick won a scholarship to a local community college, and I was $100,000 closer to achieving my educational goals and fulfilling all my life-long dreams at Lynn University!

My journey definitely wasn't easy, and there were plenty of times when I felt like retiring from the game in defeat. But I stuck it out, and didn't let my grades or the negative opinions of others stand in my way.

Thanks to my scholarship winnings during high school and beyond, I didn't have to work to support myself as I attended college. But I decided that I *wanted* to work, not for myself, but to assist other kids in finding their own path to a brighter future. As a college freshman, I began Urban

Excellence, a company designed to help students like you learn how to maximize their scholarship eligibility. The success of my Urban Excellence project has allowed me the opportunity to speak at events all across the nation, where I've had the privilege of sharing my story with the world. My hope is for this book to reach an even wider audience of "C" students and urge them to never give up on seeking the money they need for a college.

---

*For those of you who are wondering what became of my brother after Mom's ultimatum, I must admit that he won a small amount of scholarship money to attend Florida International University. My brother has "laughed" his way to becoming a successful filmmaker and stand-up comic living in San Francisco. He's also a YouTube superstar with millions of viewers. You can check out his crazy videos by searching for Will Hatcher. I'm so proud of my little bro'.

Chapter One
Sprinting Off the Starting Line

If you are like most people—including me—you've probably waited until your senior year of high school to start seriously considering applying for college scholarships. If you're not yet a senior, but you are reading this book: CONGRATULATIONS! Give yourself a pat on the back for being proactive…or, better yet, thank the adult who is *probably* behind your ownership of this scholarship guide, whether it be your financially-challenged parents, or Great-Aunt Jean who always insists on mailing you a dumb book every birthday when an iTunes-gift card would fit so much better inside of a card.

As a freshman, I was given a chance to get a jump start on my scholarship journey, but I wasted the opportunity. It all happened in a class called "Life Skills."

The course was taught by our school's soccer coach, who was the coolest guy ever. Still, even his excellent teaching didn't make up for the boring application. My grades had slacked off and I was recommended to take this vocational class but my main reason for signing up was because my boyfriend was enrolled. Hey, I was a 14-year-old girl, and we have our priorities!

As one of our assignments, our Life Skills instructor Mr. Sicard asked us to fill out this really intense, six-page scholarship application form. We were required to collect our parents' financial information, record all of our community service work to date, get three letters of recommendation, and write FIVE whole essays! My classmates were outraged, because not only was the assignment too hard, but they also considered a "practice" scholarship essay to be an entirely pointless endeavor. None of them even planned to attend college! As for me, I dutifully did the work, and then shoved my completed assignment somewhere and forgot all about it… until my senior year.

When I began filling out scholarship applications "for real," I realized that much of what they asked for was the same stuff I'd already done years ago in my Life Skills class. I literally tore apart my bedroom looking for that paperwork I'd completed as a freshman. When I finally found the old application, the contents proved to be an invaluable resource as I applied for my current scholarships. Not much about my life had changed. I still loved television production, which I took as an elective all through high school, and working in television was still my career goal. I was also involved with the same community service projects that I had worked on during my freshman year, except, by then, I had clocked many, many additional hours. Although I didn't know it at the time, all the hard, seemingly useless work I'd been forced to do during my first year of high school, really helped me to prepare for the insane scholarship game I played as a senior. Oh, and I should also mention that the scholarship application our Life Skills teacher required us to fill out just happened to be for the Communities and Schools Scholarship.

Are You Still A Freshman? Lucky You!

Why wait? The four years stretching endlessly between NOW and your eventual college career may seem like *forever*, but you'll be surprised at how fast time flies. Before you know it, some university will be thrusting out its greedy palm and demanding that you hand over a hefty stack of tuition money. What some people don't realize is that you don't need to wait until your senior year to start earning that cash. Your scholarship options will be more limited if you are a high school freshman, but such opportunities are certainly far from non-existent. Even a kindergarten student can win college money these days, so if you have your little brother's best interests in mind, you will yank the crayon out of his nose and send him to the kitchen to concoct an entry to the *Jif® Most Creative Peanut Butter Sandwich Contest.*

Those of you who know all along that you will need scholarship money can begin preparing in advance to place yourselves at an incredible advantage over your future competitors. For one thing, by thinking ahead you might see the value in working your way up the ranks from C-student to a senior with a solid B-average…but extra studying may not be the best use of your time. You've probably already accepted that you are in no mental condition to compete with the academic overachievers, so your most successful strategy may be to concentrate on having fun during your high school years. Yes, you heard me correctly: HAVE FUN!

Okay, not *too* much fun. Before I start getting angry e-mails from parents, let me stress that I am only condoning the type of "fun" that comes from participating in wholesome extracurricular activities and performing community service work that you enjoy. When you are not entering the scholarship game equipped with awesome grades, you will need to fall back on other just-as-important attributes, such as a life full of experiences and insights. While it is important to remain true to yourself and engage in only those ventures that fill you with a sense of passion, there's no reason why you can't explore a few non-scholastic activities that are fun AND will look good on your college scholarship applications. If, as a freshman, you don't feel quite ready to jump headfirst into the scholarship game, there are still two keywords you can use while preparing to win lots of money in the future: PLANNING and PRACTICE.

SPOILER ALERT!!!! As I talk about "Planning" and "Practice," I will briefly outline many of the scholarship application components that will be discussed in much more depth as the book continues. Think of this chapter as a preview of coming attractions.

Planning for Scholarships

For "C" students, it's all about increasing your eligibility for scholarships. As the age-old idiom goes: "Forewarned is forearmed." If you have no expectation of suddenly inheriting a million dollars or stumbling upon a pirate's treasure trove during your family vacation to the Caribbean, then it's a smart idea to start engineering yourself an exciting life that will put a satisfied grin on the faces of the scholarship judges.

Realizing Your Unique Potential

You possess a multitude of qualities that make you a cool and special person! It's a smart idea to figure out what these are, because you'll need to call your own personal strengths into action when you begin looking and applying for scholarships.

It might be helpful to sit down and write out a list of your talents, hobbies, extracurricular activities, personality traits, and any other unique attributes that might give you an edge when you fill out those scholarship applications. Everything about you is worth *something*.

Take a look down your list and think of ways to expand upon and enhance the talents you already have to make them even more impressive. Do you enjoy wakeboarding behind your family's speed boat in the summertime? You might consider joining an association called *USA Water Ski*. Not only will this membership help you to get more involved with the sport and improve your skills, but there are also scholarships that are open only to members. Even if you never apply for a scholarship that is geared specifically toward wakeboarders, scholarship committees of all types will be impressed by your enthusiasm for the sport!

Broadening Your Opportunities

As you do further research scholarships, you will discover that many of them have specific requirements for eligibility. For example, you can only apply if you are in foster care or if you have followed the steps necessary to receive the *Girl Scout Gold Award*. If you are planning far enough ahead, you will have the option of engineering your life in a way that will lend itself to greater scholarship opportunities. Obviously, you cannot change your ethnicity or health status, and although there may be some great scholarships offered to Amish students, it is not recommended that you abruptly switch religions and start driving a horse and buggy to school. That's just plain bad karma...well, it is if your CURRENT religion believes in such things. Otherwise, I'm sure that *all* doctrines/deities would consider a last-minute conversion just to win money a form of "cheating."

You can use scholarship search engines to get an overview of those qualities that you don't have yet, but that you can possibly develop with a little bit of extra effort. The key is to stay true to yourself and make decisions that will lead you to a happy and passion-filled life. Even within this framework you may find there are ways to mold yourself into a scholarship-winning machine.

In your hunt for college money, starting early and doing some research will open up more scholarship doors by providing hints on how to:

- Join the right clubs/associations

- Work for the right employers

- Volunteer for the right community services

- Attend the right college

- Make the right career choice

- Belong to the right fraternity or sorority

Test the Dedication of Your Parents

As you explore the scholarships you will prepare yourself to apply for in the future, don't overlook the opportunities you can glean by getting your parents involved in your planning. As a matter of fact, two of the scholarships that I won were because my parents were members of organizations. My dad was a member of the Fraternity Phi Beta Sigma and my mother was in the Classroom Teachers Association.

After perusing the Internet, you will realize that many of the clubs and associations with scholarship programs are not organizations that any young person off the street can sign up for and join. YOU may not have the correct qualifications to get involved, but your parents might! Ask your parents about their employer benefits, work unions, and social clubs. If your parents belong to some of the right ones already—great! If not, ask them if there are any helpful associations that they are eligible to join.

You'll know that your parents really care about your education if they are willing to do any of the following:

○ Switch employers to provide you with better scholarship opportunities

○ Move to a different state to provide you with better scholarship opportunities

○ Join the military to provide you with better scholarship opportunities

Start laying on guilt now, and who knows what you'll ultimately talk your parents into?

Suck Up to the Right Adults

An important part of your scholarship application packet will be Letters of Recommendation from teachers, clergy members, neighbors, and other people who know and love you. I'll be talking about this more in Chapter Five, but now is the time to start looking around and noticing any available adults who you think will be able to write flattering and impressive things about you. If your adult of choice does not know and/or like you yet, you've got a few years to start sucking up and getting yourself noticed. If this adult *does* like you, make sure that your relationship remains strong and positive.

Here is a list of people that you can approach to write you a recommendation letter:

○ Employer

○ Community Service Rep

○ Coach

- ○ Neighbor

- ○ Teacher

- ○ Principal

- ○ Church Official

- ○ Coworker

- ○ Guidance Counselor

- ○ Probation Officer (Just kidding…unless you really have one)

Show the adults in your life that you are an upstanding young citizen, and they will be tripping over each other as they line up to help you win money for college. Suck up until it hurts…but remember that you only need to be nice to a half dozen or so people. The rest will have to fend for themselves and this includes your parents, because they can't give you recommendation letters.

Practicing for Scholarships

There are many steps in the process of being awarded a scholarship, but students who get started early will have a chance to practice the skills they will need to become successful scholarship applicants.

Organization

It's never too soon to learn how to organize both your time and your school materials. If you intend to apply for multiple scholarships at one time, it is essential that you develop an organized system to keep all of your paperwork in order (more about this in Chapter Six). If you begin practicing and perfecting your organizational skills as you begin high school, you may even find that your grades improve, along with your chances of winning a scholarship.

Applications

Every scholarship you apply for will begin with an application (more about these in Chapter Three). The best way to practice for filling out scholarship applications is to complete *actual* scholarship applications and submit them to the sponsoring organization. If you don't win, it's no big problem—you have several more years to keep trying, and the practice alone will do you good.

You can also hone your application skills by collecting and filling them out for job opportunities in your area. If you need a part-time job, you'll be doing this anyway, but even if you don't want a job, gathering the necessary information and filling out the job application forms will be useful practice for later. Want to practice now? Practice applications are available on the "C" Student's Rock website on www.cstudentsrock.com

Interviews

Going out on job interviews is even more valuable than merely filling out the applications. If you are a finalist for a scholarship award, you will very likely be invited to interview before the judging committee (more about this in Chapter Seven). Any practice you can get conducting yourself maturely and answering difficult questions with poise and dignity will be highly beneficial to you later on.

Obviously, you can't go to interviews if you do not intend to accept the job, so your realistic experiences may be limited, especially if you are offered the first position that you interview for! To get more practice, you can always stage "fake" interviews and go through the steps of dressing up, submitting your resume, and undergoing interrogation. Of course, this type of role-playing will be more relaxed than the real thing and probably won't help you learn to cope with butterflies in your tummy. You may even find yourself struggling to hold back your laughter when your best friend or your big brother arrives dressed up in Dad's over-sized suit and begins asking you serious questions. If you want to practice in a more accurate, yet still pretend setting, talk to your parents about asking their bosses to conduct a simulated interview in their workplace on your behalf.

Essays

Essay writing is a part of nearly every scholarship application, so it's in your best interest to learn how to do it well (more about this in Chapter Four). If you want to "just get by" with a passing grade in mathematics or art, be my guest, but chug an energy drink and walk into your English class prepared to pay attention and learn!

Chances are that you will be required to write many essays throughout your high school career. Embrace this opportunity and take to heart any corrections or criticism that your teachers provide. Feeling confident about your ability to compose an effective essay will take much of the trauma out of the most painful component of your scholarship application packet. If you plan correctly, you may not even need to write a fresh, new essay when the time comes to "wow" the scholarship judges. Read up on common essay topics and use those questions as subjects for your English assignments whenever possible. These essays will be thoroughly critiqued and evaluated, so you will know how to improve them for submission with your scholarship applications.

Careers

It really is good practice to consider what you want to do with your life as early as possible, but don't worry that the decisions you make as a high school freshman will lock you into a single, non-negotiable career. Remember in kindergarten when you swore you wanted to be a ballerina or astronaut? I bet nobody held you to *that* promise! The same leniency applies later in life. You can always change educational paths, even if you've already begun studying a specific subject (with or without a scholarship).

As you read this book, you will find many references to my own goal to make a career for myself in television production. If you've read my author bio, you know that this dream never became reality. It wasn't that I failed in my mission; I just changed my mind during the course of my college education, and enrolled in a different program of study that I found more interesting and useful. Still, despite the end result, my passion and dedication for television production served me well as I applied for college scholarships. The judges like to see young people with achievable goals and strong commitment, so just pick a career and go with it. If the choice turns out to be the wrong one for you, switch gears later.

Once you've decided on a career to experiment with, look for ways to practice the skills you'll need for that particular job through part-time work, community service, or internships. This will serve as an example of your dedication, and help you out considerably when applying for scholarships that are offered to students entering that specific course of study. Let's say you've decided that you'd like to teach elementary school as a career. When you apply for scholarships open only to future educators, you want to be able to say more than just, "I want to be a teacher because I love children and I think it would be fun to be around them all day." It will be far more impressive if you can list the actual EXPERIENCES that you've had working with kids, such as teaching swimming lessons during the summer, or volunteering your time to help underprivileged grade-schoolers with their homework. The scholarship committee will feel more confident about awarding you money if they have evidence of your success and happiness in the career field of your choice.

Okay, now you have a few new ideas for how to prepare yourself for entry into the scholarship game, unless it's already too late for that (yes, seniors, I'm talking to you!). But whether you are an eager freshman/sophomore or a desperate junior/senior, I'm guessing that you're getting anxious to hear about the good stuff. In the next chapter, I will tell you how to hunt down those scholarships that will help you to achieve your dreams!

Notes

Notes

_____

_____

_____

_____

_____

_____

_____

_____

_____

_____

_____

_____

_____

_____

_____

_____

_____

_____

_____

_____

_____

_____

_____

_____

_____

_____

Chapter Two
Show Me the Money!

Let's Be Realistic...

...stick to the scholarships that you might actually win. There's nothing at all wrong with remaining optimistic, but applying for a scholarship that you are not qualified to receive is just a waste of everybody's time. Before you square your shoulders and stride off on a quest to seek out and conquer the ultimate scholarship, pause and take a moment to answer these questions—out loud or in your head, I don't care which.

1. Have you ever had an award presented to you by the President of the United States or any other world leader?

2. Did your high school teachers unanimously decide to award you grades of 5.0, because 4.0 just wasn't good enough?

3. Has one of your inventions ever saved a starving village during a drought and/or famine?

4. Have you ever scored in excess of 100 points per game in any sport (golf does not count)?

5. Did you compose your first piano concerto while wearing a pair of Huggies Pull-ups®?

6. Has CNN ever done a news story about your accomplishments that did not begin with the words, "The fire chief traced the source of the inferno to…"?

7. Have you discovered the cure for *any* kind of cancer (even an obscure type)?

8. Did you play the lead in your school's fall production so brilliantly that Will Smith showed up for the final performance, and then

asked if you would co-star with him in his next blockbuster movie?

9. Do you think that I'm grossly exaggerating the expected accomplishments of a high school student to make you feel like a loser?

10. Are you ready to work hard to find scholarships that you can realistically win, then do all the tedious steps it takes to fill out and submit the applications in time?

If you could not answer "Yes" to any of the first eight questions... congratulations! You are a NORMAL person, despite what your sibling has been telling you all these years. Unfortunately, your normality will probably exclude you from winning any huge national scholarships with a virtual parade of zeros following the first number. I'll cheer you on if you want to try, but don't feel too disappointed if you fail to win a National Merit Scholarship Award. Remember, I warned you.

If you answered "Yes" to question #10, then good for you! This attitude is all you really need to succeed in the scholarship game, so READ ON!

Okay, So What Kind of Scholarships Should You Apply For?

I'm advising you against relying on a single, gigantic scholarship that will sail you through your entire college career, so what is a regular, normal kid like you *supposed* to do? What kinds of scholarships are realistically attainable for someone who likes playing *Angry Birds* on his iPhone more than he likes computing the square root of a negative number on his scientific calculator?

Don't despair! There ARE scholarships available to you and all other non-super students living among us, but you'll need to do some research to hunt down the right ones. Even if you think you have nothing to offer a scholarship committee, you might be surprised at what you can find. I remember once when I was doing volunteer work in a school career center, helping to match students with appropriate scholarships, a girl came in and sifted through the scholarship offerings that were on display, and then turned to leave the center with a look of discouragement on her face. I stopped her by asking, "Is there a specific type of scholarship I can help you find?"

"No," the girl replied sadly. "I already looked, and there's just *nothing*. My grades are bad and I'm not good at sports or anything like that, so nobody will want to give me money for college."

I was determined to prove to this girl that she didn't need to be a super achiever to win a scholarship and I did! I found her an application for a scholarship that *anybody* could apply for; the organization only asked that each contender write an essay about bees. There were no other eligibility requirements. She didn't have to be an amateur beekeeper, she didn't have to be allergic to stings, she didn't have to eat honey for every meal—she only had to write an essay on the broad topic of buzzing insects. This put the girl on the same level as every other high school kid who hardly ever thinks about bees. She wrote her essay and she won the scholarship!

Granted, a successful bee essay probably will not generate a big enough award to foot your entire college bill. You may not be able to pay your tuition with one massive scholarship, but the smaller ones do add up if you apply for and win multiple awards, like I did. Also, the more scholarship victories you achieve, the more opportunities you have to hit your parents up for a congratulatory dinner at your favorite restaurant. Use the ideas offered in this chapter to find and pursue the types of scholarships that YOU are qualified to win!

Get Local

At the end of the movie *The Wizard of Oz*, Dorothy says "… *if I ever go looking for my heart's desire again, I won't look any further than my own backyard.*" Learn from the girl's mistakes, and before you head out battling "wizards" (4.0 students) and "witches" (cranky people who spend so much time padding their scholarship-winning resumes that they never have time to relax and enjoy life), first take a look around your own backyard. Local scholarships are abundant and naturally will put you up against a smaller number of competitors than the awards that are nationally known and advertised. Many of these scholarships may be somewhat obscure, and more or less free for the taking to anyone diligent enough to dig them up. You may not realize it, but no matter where you live, you are literally surrounded by potential scholarship opportunities! For example, your local pizza franchise might participate in the Papa John's Scholars program, and if you win one of their awards, you'll experience the added thrill of having your scholarship check delivered to you in a pizza box! What's the one thing better than pizza? Major money for college, of course!

Check with any and all of the following to inquire about possible scholarship offerings:

- Clubs you join

- Organizations you volunteer with

- Your employer

- Your parents' employers

- Associations that your parents belong to

- Your place of worship

- Businesses in your area

Although I applied for many of the big, national scholarships (Duracell, Bill and Melinda Gates, Discover Card), I ultimately found my own success in local competitions. The first step to finding local scholarships is to do a quick Google search.

Do a quick Google search using the following:

Scholarships + [Insert the name of your city or state]

Write your top three leads here:

1._____

2._____

3._____

Get Specific

Some individuals or organizations narrow down the number of people who are eligible for their scholarships by offering them to only a specific type of individual. Some of these awards may be highly competitive (not to say that YOU won't be the winner), but you might be lucky enough to discover an award that is just so perfectly tailored to you, that there's no chance of you NOT winning the money. Take the example of the oh-so-fortunate Zolp family tree. Any person lucky enough to be born with this uncommon last name and who is a Catholic receives a free ride at Loyola University in Chicago. Okay, so your name isn't Zolp (or it IS, but you're a Presbyterian). No problem, there's also scholarships offered to people with the surnames Valkenburg, Gatling, and Scarpinato.

Typically, such specificity in scholarships out there is reserved for a more logical purpose. The American Welding Society, for example, offers a scholarship geared toward young people wishing to launch their own career in—you guessed it—welding! Many groups, organizations, or specialty colleges are eager to educate people who share their same interests and passions. Other scholarships are set up by individuals or in honor of individuals who exhibit a certain trait. For example, Horatio Alger, Jr. wrote books about poor street boys who struggled but succeeded at raising their station in life. In tribute to this deceased 1800's author, The Horatio Alger Association of Distinguished Americans provides scholarships to low-income students who demonstrate commitment and a drive for overcoming adversity. Likewise, other philanthropists might seek out scholarship recipients who match criteria that they find appealing.

When beginning your scholarship search, scrutinize yourself to determine which of your personal characteristics are special and distinct enough to qualify you for "exclusive" scholarship options. Be sure to consider:

- Your hobbies
- Your talents
- Your athletic activities
- Your ethnicity
- Your religion
- Your career choice
- Your choice of schools
- Your military affiliation
- Your medical status
- Everything else (i.e., hair color, right handedness/left handedness, height, study habits)

I have compiled a few lists of interesting scholarships that demonstrate how enterprising students can take advantage of their extra-special specialness and win themselves money for college. Of course, you are a very special person yourself, but don't be disappointed if you aren't qualified to receive very many of the awards listed below. Just keep looking until you uncover a scholarship that is perfect for you!

Physical Attributes

Forget being born a boring ol' genius. You can also be eligible for scholarships based on the less-useful genes that your parents passed down to you. Here are some examples of organizations that offer scholarships for people with "special" (I did NOT say freakish, so don't send hate-mail!) physical attributes.

- If you are really tall, contact Tall Clubs International.

- If you under four feet, ten inches, try The Little People of America.

- If you are larger than life, you might get college money from the National Association to Advance Fat Acceptance.

- If you are not quite one-of-a-kind, check out the advantages of the Furlotte Twins Endowed Scholarship.

- If you are turning the pages of this book with your left hand, you can apply for The Frederick and Mary F. Beckley Scholarship.

Bizarre Talents

"Why am I 'wasting my time with this nonsense,' Dad? I'll tell you why. My crazy hobby just might pay for my college education one day." Kids exactly like you have won scholarships for their prowess at everything from hustling a good game of pool to playing the bagpipes like a true Scotsman (okay, maybe not kids *exactly* like you). You could win a scholarship for people with bizarre talents simply by

- **Quacking** convincingly enough to win The Chick and Sophie Major Memorial scholarship for duck-calling.

- **Building** your fake stock portfolio quicker than other wanna-be investors to secure the Excellence in Predicting the Future Award.

- **Baking** the most ultimately patriotic apple pie for the Culinary Institute of America scholarship.

○ **Knocking** down enough pins to earn acclaim with The United States Bowling Congress.

○ **Knitting** something truly spectacular to enter into the National Make It Yourself with Wool competition.

○ **Shooting** with precise aim to win a scholarship at the National Marbles Tournament.

Unique Interest

Maybe you are considered too weird to secure a date to the prom, but being your own free-spirited self just might give you an advantage in the scholarship game! Some examples of ways that your unique interests could win you a scholarship are by:

○ **Being** so enthralled by the *Poltergeist* and *Paranormal Activity* movie franchises that you are inspired to apply for a Parapsychology Foundation scholarship.

○ **Loving** every potato-related product from Tater Tots to Mr. Potato Head toys so much that you want to study tuber-growing on behalf of the National Potato Council.

○ **Appreciating** linguistics—both in and out-of-this-world—enough to win the Kor Memorial Scholarship from the Klingon Language Institute.

○ **Being** passionate enough about an animal's right to live beyond dinner time to satisfy the hunger of The Vegetarian Resource Group.

○ **Disliking** the person who won the vegetarian scholarship so much that you join The National Beef Ambassador Program.

○ **Loving** the melodic sound of Beethoven"s music ricocheting off your school gym walls enough to write a winning essay for The School Band and Orchestra Magazine Scholarship.

○ **Having** such an insatiable sweet tooth that you qualify to win the American Association of Candy Technologist's John Kitt Memorial Scholarship.

○ **Being** so crazy for fuzzy llamas that you are a shoe-in for a scholarship from The Michigan Llama Association.

○ **Feeling** uninhibited enough to win a scholarship offered by the American Association of Nude Recreation or the American Nudist Research Library.

If you don't happen to possess any of the above interests, check out what's happening on the Common Knowledge Scholarship Foundation (www.cksf.org) website. This organization offers monthly online quizzes on a wide variety of obscure topics. If you score high on an initial quiz, you will advance to the next level with a chance of winning the championship round! At the time of writing this book, scholarships were being offered to students who knew facts about Homeland Security, personal finance, and the laws of cyberspace. Who knows, maybe one of next month's quizzes will be about the very subject that YOU have been researching since kindergarten!

Get Creative

You may not have an awesome overall GPA, but that doesn't mean that you aren't brilliant in a few selected scholarly areas. You might have gotten an F in history because you spent all your homework time trying to figure out a formula that would break the time-space continuum and allow you to turn your broken water heater into a working time machine. Someone with such ambitious aspirations is *not* dumb, and even if your invention never successfully launches, you could win a scholarship by writing a fictional story about your ultimate trip back in time and entering it into L. Ron Hubbard's Writers and Illustrators of the Future Contest. For less Star Trekking creative writers, look for scholarships that are awarded solely on the quality of your essay, without taking into account your grades or SAT score. This was a strategy I used to great success. One example for high school students in the District of Columbia area is the Washington Regional Transplant Community annual essay competition on the topic of organ and tissue donation.

If you don't write fiction yourself, but love to read and analyze the works of others, enter scholarship contests offered by The Ayn Rand Institute or publishing houses like Penguin and Avar Press. If you can prove a hypothesis like a pro, the Intel Science Talent Search is a good option for showing off your skills and winning college money.

If you are a budding artist, it won't be too hard to find scholarship committees eager to view your visual masterpieces, but even the non-traditional artistic types stand a chance in the scholarship game. Get your fingers sticky while designing elegant evening wear out of duct tape, and not only will you look stunning at your school dance, but you could win big money in Duck Brand's yearly Stuck At Prom® competition.

Ever feel like you're channeling the ghost of Ed Wood? In this multimedia age, internet video competitions have become very popular, so why not say, "I want to direct." You can win all sorts of things by writing a clever script and turning yourself into a star, but the best prizes are large college scholarships! Get out your digital camcorder and film a short clip to enter the SimpleLeap Flashcard Scholarship Competition or Dr. Pepper's Million Dollar Tuition Giveaway. Famous talk show host and former C-student, David Letterman, will give you $10,000 to attend the telecommunications program at his alma mater if you can make him laugh hard enough with your video to his scholarship contest. A sign outside the door of the audio studio at Ball State University reads "To All C-Students Before Me and After Me—David Letterman." A true inspiration!

Get Lucky (But Don't Count On It)

Unless you were raised by gorillas in the African Congo, you've probably seen, entered, and NOT won dozens of billion-dollar sweepstakes by now. Good thing, too, because if you weren't 18 years old when you entered the contest, the prize would have been immediately yanked out of your hands. But guess what? When you *are* 18, you probably STILL won't win!

Take a look around and you will see that there are sweepstakes for new cars, luxurious vacations, and $100,000 shopping sprees. The same is true for scholarships. In fact, there is *a lot* of scholarship money given away on the Internet. I'm not going to list all the current contests (they come and go, of course), because you'll find them easily enough yourself, but before your pupils turn into dollar signs, let me share with you—The Three Worst Plans for Financing Your College Education:

1. Hope that a man with a strange accent will one day show up and reveal your true identity as the long-lost prince of a small, but wealthy, nation. Use the vast treasury to pay your college tuition.

2. Save a billionaire's baby from being eaten by a dingo. Accept tuition to the college of your choice as a reward of gratitude.

3. Count on winning a massive jackpot from one of the online scholarship sweepstakes.

While none of the above scenarios are very likely to happen, you'd be stupid to turn them down if they DID happen! Don't call the cops on that strange man and have him arrested for stalking, and, by all means SAVE THAT BABY. Even if the kid's parents are poor, you may be able to sell your story to *Reader's Digest.* And since somebody has to win those college scholarships (there's a law, I'm pretty sure), it's worth entering just on the slim chance that the winner might be you. I can guarantee that the prize money will be well worth the time it took you to fill out the entry form! P.S.: Have a back-up plan, just in case your name is never drawn out of that hat.

Does the idea of money for nothing make you feel like a lazy good-for-nothing? Good news! Some scholarship lotteries make you work for and earn your unlikely chance to win tuition dollars. Here are some examples:

Firesprinkler.org—Read about fire sprinklers. Take an easy 10-question quiz. Be rewarded with one sweepstakes entry per correct answer. Hope your name is drawn.

Zinch.com—Write about the provided topic in the website's weekly "Three Sentence Essay Sweepstakes." Answer more questions about yourself. Be entered in the lottery drawing. Hope your name is drawn.

ScholarshipPoints.com—Register for the website. Earn points by doing "fun, simple activities." Exchange your points for entries into the scholarship lotteries of your choice. Hope your name is drawn.

If you're interested in ways to gamble for scholarships that give better odds, Zinch.com's Refer-A-Dweeb program advertises that if you invite your friends to join their free website, and any of *them* win a scholarship, YOU will be awarded the same amount (until they've given away a pre-set amount of money for the year). Got smart and talented friends? Get busy sending invitations!

Another way to make bank off of your friends is to participate on CollegeNET.com's student forums. Be nice, and get the other people on the board to like you. Each week, whichever member has received the most popularity "votes" wins a nice-sized scholarship (amounts vary). This is better social networking than Facebook, because nobody ever begs you to adopt an orphaned baby cow like they do when you play Farmville. Oh, and because you can get college money for having lots and lots of loyal friends.

Where Should You Hunt For Scholarships?

Schools

Well, the first place to start would be your own high school. Chances are that you show up there at least occasionally, so why not drop by the career center while you're there? This may be the best source for learning about those really cool local scholarships that I recommended earlier.

Also, ask your guidance counselor and/or your favorite teachers if they've heard of any scholarship competitions that seem right for you. If you are determined to seek out every single available scholarship, it might be a good idea to visit some *other* high school career centers in your area, just to see if they've got anything new and different that your own faculty missed.

The college of your choice is another great place to find scholarships. When you are browsing the Internet or visiting universities, inquire about any school-specific scholarships that you might qualify to apply for. And if you aren't picky about what college you eventually attend, your scholarship options will broaden substantially!

The Internet

In today's wonderful world of technology and instant information, finding an abundance of well-known scholarships is as easy as typing a few keywords into Google's search engine. Cyberspace is home to numerous absolutely free databases that will list—and even help you organize and manage—hundreds of available scholarships. Each of these sites works on a variation of a system where you:

1. Log in (or not).

2. Enter lots of information about yourself (or just a little).

3. Generate a list of scholarships that you qualify to win (or scroll through a standard list).

4. Save a collection of your favorite scholarships (write them down, if the site doesn't have this feature yet).

5. Click to learn more information (or to be transferred to the organization's own website).

6. Apply for your scholarships right there online (when available).

There is an Index of Web Resources at the end of this book where I provide detailed reviews of the many Internet scholarship search engines that are currently active on the Web. But before you get too excited and break your mouse double-clicking like a maniac, I must first warn you about a few obstacles you might need to navigate during your online quest for college money:

1. Many of the sites require you to create an account and sign in using a valid e-mail address. Any time that you share e-mail account information, you run the risk of being barraged with spam and/or legitimate messages from the administrators. It is

also sometimes difficult to unsubscribe once your name is on a list. If you don't want to jeopardize the sanctity of your main inbox, it might be a good idea to set up a free email account specifically to use during your scholarship hunt. I recommend a user name such as YourName_Scholarships@....

2. If you don't want a lot of junk flooding into your NEW account, stay observant during the sign-up process and click the boxes to opt out of receiving additional promotional e-mails.

3. Websites need a source of revenue to survive, and primarily the hosts depend on ad links to make ends meet. There's no harm in this. You come to their site to look at scholarship lists; the owners make money just because you were there seeing the advertisements on the page. It's a win-win scenario for all. Still, always beware of false created to direct you to places that you don't necessarily want to go. Many scholarship search sites are affiliated with a loan company or some similar business, and exist merely to expose you to their own products/services. There is no harm in this, either, but the self-promoting can sometimes reach very annoying levels of extremity.

4. Many scholarship search engines are not kept up-to-date. Don't get excited about the perfect opportunity until you determine that the advertised scholarship is not already a week (or several years) past its deadline for submissions.

5. Don't expect too much from the "customized list" of scholarships given to you based on the facts that you entered about yourself. The technology to edit awards that you are unqualified to receive is primitive, at best. You will invariably be ineligible for half the scholarships displayed on your screen! Experiment with adding/deleting information within your profile and observe the resulting changes (if any). or stick to websites that allow you to browse their ENTIRE scholarship list independently.

While you are browsing the Internet, try simple keyword combinations to catch less well-known opportunities that the big databases may have overlooked. Try entering the word "scholarship" along with your town, your county, your state, your dream college, etc.

Scholarship "Yellow Pages"

If you are the old-fashioned type who would rather squint at words on a page rather than words on your computer screen, check your local library or bookstore for one of the annually published scholarship compilations. These massive volumes contain a vast array of scholarship titles, along with details about eligibility and how to obtain further information. The listings are first grouped into categories, and then presented in alphabetical order according to name. These books are only an initial step in the process of finding a scholarship, as they lack the convenience of providing you with an instant application, but the books are the best resource for browsing through literally thousands of scholarships all compiled into one place. Just be prepared to skim over several pages of awards you are ineligible to receive between discovering each viable possibility. Oh, and have a magnifying glass standing by, because the print in these books is very, very tiny.

Your Personal "Scholarship Network"

"Ask and ye shall receive!"

This is either a quote from the Bible or the motto of a pirate gang...but probably the former, because pirates tend to pillage towns and take stuff without asking. Whatever the case, don't be shy about telling everybody you know that you are on a mission to apply for every scholarship you can find. Ask around for ideas, and request your friends and family to keep a lookout on your behalf. Your Aunt Marge might prove to be a valuable resource when she nominates you for her flower club's "Blossoming Student of the Year," award!

Where NOT to Look For Scholarships

You should never have to PAY anybody to help you find scholarships. This game is about increasing your college fund, not decreasing it! Some companies out there will charge you a fee for the "service" of assisting you in your scholarship search. They might make promises like:

○ "We GUARANTEE that our clients will win a scholarship!"

○ "We'll do all the work; you just sit back and relax!"

○ "We know about scholarships that can't be found anywhere else!"

○ "We've got a secret list of scholarships that always go unclaimed!"

○ "We'll refund your money if you aren't satisfied!"

Despite these inflated claims, and even with the very best of intentions, no service company can guarantee anybody a scholarship. At least, not a good one! If they have a scholarship-or-your-money-back guarantee, they can probably find you a fifty-buck prize (even if they have to award it to you themselves), which will justify them in keeping the $300 "finder's fee" you paid. Getting a refund for sketchy service is never as easy as returning a too-small pair of jeans to Wal-Mart!

Even if someone else is willing to take the information you've given them and fill-out/mail/manage your scholarship entries, do you really want to give up that control? Are they also going to write your essay for you?

You can do your own scholarship search with a plethora of results—you don't need to pay anyone else to type a few words into an Internet search engine. No, this company does not have a CIA-style intelligence team ferreting out scholarships that have been hidden in the depths of Pakistani caves. If you feel like you need some help during your scholarship hunt, there are plenty of people and/or organizations that will help you for FREE.

In the vast majority of cases, there is no charge to apply for or "hold" a scholarship. If you are ever asked to spend money up front for a chance to win a scholarship, listen to that voice inside your head that is screaming "SCAM!" Before paying any scholarship related fees check your sources carefully and make sure that the charge is legitimate.

Should I Ever Pursue a Scholarship That Doesn't Seem Right for Me?

If you are ineligible for the scholarship, then my answer is "No." You will be wasting your own valuable time, not to mention the time of the committee member who must preview your application before throwing it into the reject heap. Read all scholarship requirements and directions very carefully, and make sure you are eligible before you send in the application. Apply ONLY for scholarships that you stand a chance of winning.

If you are eligible, but unlikely to win the scholarship, then my answer is "Maybe." There is never any harm in trying, of course, unless filling out the iffy application will interfere with or prevent you from applying for scholarships that are better suited to your strengths.

If you can make the scholarship right for you, then my answer is a resounding, "Yes!" If you are ineligible to apply because you've never performed volunteer work overseas, for instance, and your church is planning a mission trip to Honduras, for example, then you should arrange to go along and help. After you return home safely to your video games and Oreo cookies, you can apply for the scholarship that you've now made right for you. You can't always wait around for the perfect opportunity to fall into your lap. Sometimes, you have to create the opportunity or open up your own door to qualify.

Whether or not you intend to apply, you should still pick up every scholarship application that you come across. Save them in a file somewhere, because throughout the course of your education you will continue to gain experiences, skills, group affiliations, etc. When you look through your collection of rejected applications later, you just may find that you qualify for a wider variety of scholarships than you did back at the beginning of your quest. Never forget that most scholarship competitions are held annually, and are often open to a wide variety of age groups. If you aren't eligible during your senior year of high school, re-evaluate your qualifications as a college freshman.

Finding His Creative Niche:
Channing's Scholarship Story

"Action!"

On cue, Bobby, who was playing the role of a homicide detective, began to brutishly interrogate Channing's little brother about the sudden disappearance of "Flashcard Man."

"Did you torture him first, you creep?" Bobby shouted. When the suspect refused to speak, his interrogator continued to scream at him.

"What did you do?"

"Did you torture him first, you sicko?"

"Tell me!"

"Did you torture him first, you creep?"

"Cut, cut!" said an exasperated Channing as he lowered his camera. "You already said creep. This time it's supposed to be, 'Did you torture him first, you ANIMAL?'"

"I wish you'd remember your lines, Bobby," Channing's brother, Jonfranco, complained. "We're going to be here forever if you keep screwing stuff up."

"This from the kid who's only got ONE little line in the entire movie," Bobby shot back. "Even a parrot could be trained to say, 'No, I recycled him,' so just shut up before I make you switch parts with me."

"Nobody's switching parts," Channing interjected quickly. "You know we don't have time to be messing around. I've got to get this film edited and submitted to the SimpleLeap scholarship competition in just three days, so let's focus people!"

"Lay off. It's not our fault you waited until the last minute," Jonfranco muttered.

"There's not enough time to do this right," Bobby added. "Maybe we should just forget the whole thing?"

Channing and his crew almost did quit without entering the competition. Channing had learned about the SimpleLeap scholarship only four days before the submission deadline. The assignment was simple enough—all he had to do was create a three-minute movie about how he got rid of his archaic flashcards after discovering SimpleLeap's more effective study software. Easy, right? Especially since Channing had both a friend and a brother who were cool enough to help him out.

But with such harsh time constraints for conceiving, scripting, filming, editing, and scoring his project, the pressure was on and stress levels were high. Lucky for Channing, he and his crew proved themselves up to the challenge of creating a masterpiece in a ridiculously short period of time. Their movie won the competition!

Like all aspiring students of higher education, Channing was worried about where he would get the tuition money for community college. Despite being ineligible to receive financial aid, Channing hadn't really considered scholarships to be a viable source of income, so he pursued them only half-heartedly. His organizational plan consisted of a simple folder on his computer desktop labeled "Scholarship Attempts" and a drawer of materials in his closet. He kept tabs on his entries by checking the status online.

Now, after winning $500 from SimpleLeap, Channing knows that scholarship applications do lead to real money. As president of the student government group at his college, he is dedicated to his education and continues to need financial help to achieve his goals. "Every once in a while a scholarship catches my attention and I go full throttle for it," Channing reports. "There are all kinds of scholarships out there that tailor to everyone's different skills, so instead of waiting for one to catch my eye, I think I'd be better off going out and finding a few."

Good advice, Channing!

Notes

Notes

_____

_____

_____

_____

_____

_____

_____

_____

_____

_____

_____

_____

_____

_____

_____

_____

_____

_____

_____

_____

_____

_____

Notes

Chapter Three
Application Do's and Don'ts

You've searched for the organizations that have scholarship money to give away, and you've singled out the ones that want to give their money to YOU...they just don't know it yet. How are you going to show these scholarship committees that you are the person who needs, deserves, and will appreciate the funding they have to offer?

When applying for scholarships, you have to become your own sales person, publicist, and hype man. It is your duty to sell yourself to people who are looking to invest their money into promising individuals. The catch is that they don't know you, and in most cases you have 500 words or less to tell them what an outstanding person you are and how much you really need their money. Scholarship awarding boils down to simple business principles. Organizations want an ROI, which in the business world means a "Return On Investment." They want to know that the person who receives their award is going to make the best of the educational opportunity and not waste their scholarship money on a half-hearted attempt to attend a class or two between toga parties. It's your job to convince the scholarship committee that you are the type of student who has a sense of personal responsibility and the determination to succeed!

The thing you need to remember as you embark upon your scholarship journey is that there IS an abundance of money ready and waiting for you...but getting it is not always easy. If it were a matter of simply signing your name on the dotted line, then *everyone* would have scholarships! Very few things in this world are truly free and that includes "free" money.

That said, scholarships are still very obtainable if you are willing to invest the time and energy necessary to complete the steps that will take you from broke to beneficiary. And it all begins with an application.

Where Do I Get My Applications?

There are a number of ways to obtain physical applications that are ready to be completed and mailed. Here are the most common means of acquiring your scholarship applications:

○ By visiting a central source, like a scholarship fair or your school's career center

○ In person, at the business location of the sponsor

○ Printing from an online database, or the website of the funding organization

○ Writing to a sponsor to request an application by mail

The first three options are self-explanatory, so all you need now are some examples of how to write a letter requesting a scholarship application from an organization. On the following pages, you will find two samples of Application Request Letters. The first version is more formal and the second is more creative. While an application request is not a "contest" you can win or lose, it doesn't hurt to put your most memorable foot forward. You never know who will read your letter, or how influential this person may be!

SAMPLE APPLICATION REQUEST LETTER #1

(Date)

(Scholarship Coordinator)

(Name of Scholarship)

(Address of Organization)

(City, State Zip)

Dear Scholarship Coordinator:

I recently learned about the (scholarship/internship/fellowship) offered by your organization. I believe I would make an ideal candidate, because... (Enter a few credible details).

Please send me an application and any other information pertaining to the (scholarship). I have enclosed a self-addressed stamped envelope for your convenience. Thank you for your assistance. I look forward to receiving the requested paperwork.

Sincerely,

(Your signature)

SAMPLE APPLICATION REQUEST LETTER #2

(Date)

(Scholarship Coordinator)

(Name of Scholarship)

(Address of Organization)

(City, State Zip)

Dear Scholarship Chairperson,

"If you chase after goals, but forget your heart, you'll be doing it for someone else." (Acura)

Rather than play hide and go seek with my priorities, I am doggedly pursuing my goals—nonstop—with my heart in every inch of what I do. This is the reason why I am writing to you.

My name is Felecia Hatcher. I am a college-bound senior at Community High School. I am on a quest for financial assistance. Please send me an application as well as an information packet about your scholarship program. With your help, I can reach my highest potential.

Respectfully Yours,

Felecia Hatcher (Signature)

(Mailing address)

Scholarship Democracy: How to Get the Nomination

Some scholarships are not open to all interested applicants, but require potential recipients to be nominated by a third party. Hopefully, you are so awesome that your teachers, neighbors, and employers are nominating you for scholarships left and right!

If not, no worries. It's simply a matter of the right people not knowing about the right scholarships. If you discover a scholarship that fits you to a tee, don't feel dejected if you discover that only nominees are eligible. All you need to do in this situation is find the right person and politely ask him/her to complete the steps for your nomination.

Who is the right person, you ask? In many cases, your nominator can be any person who knows you well enough to write a strong and persuasive letter on your behalf. Other times, the scholarship will require a certain type of nomination, and the sponsor will specify exactly who is allowed to propose a possible recipient. For example, an organization might invite high school English teachers to nominate their most talented student poet, or elderly people to suggest a young person who has selflessly offered up unsolicited assistance.

If nominations are accepted from any source, it may still be a good idea to put some thought into which person you will ask to represent you to the committee. If the scholarship is being awarded to students who have proved outstanding dedication to the community, your best representative may be the coordinator of your favorite volunteer program, rather than your pastor. If the scholarship is offered only to exceptional windsurfers, you probably want to ask your water sports coach to write the letter, not your mailman (even if you are really, really good friends with your mailman).

Ten Tips for Submitting Amazing Application Packets:

1. Make Multiple "Practice" Copies.

Before you begin excitedly scribbling all over your essay application, your first step is to make multiple photocopies of the forms. If you "screw one up," it MIGHT be a simple matter of printing out a new application from the organization's website, otherwise your mistake might turn into a total nightmare! What if you had to write to the sponsors to request the application? Will you look like a responsible and reliable person if you send out a second letter which reads like the following?

```
Dear Committee,

Please send me a fresh application for your
scholarship. I regret that when I began filling
out the forms, my mind was on this anime
cartoon that I really like to watch, and so,
without really thinking, I answered all of your
questions with Japanese characters. I apologize
for any inconvenience my mistake has caused.


Sincerely,

Felecia Hatcher


P.S. Since it is now only three days before
your deadline, I will also need an extension
on the time allowed to submit my application.
Thank you!
```

It is smart to have plenty of extra copies, so you are able to hand in the neatest, most perfect application form possible—no crossed off words and no White-Out smears!

2. Always Follow Directions!

Before you make a single mark on your application, carefully read over any and all instructions supplied for completing your packet. There may not be many specific guidelines to follow, but the list of rules and regulations could also be extensive. It all depends on the organization and its expectations.

The one thing ALL scholarship committees will expect is for their applicants to possess three basic qualities:

    a. An ability to read directions

    b. An ability to pay attention

    c. An ability to obey instructions

Many applications are thrown directly into the trash without a moment's hesitation because they are completed incorrectly. This indicates to the committee that the person applying cannot read, which is a hindrance to a successful college education; doesn't pay attention to detail, which also will affect college performance; or simply does not care about the rules and will probably be expelled from college before the first semester is over.

Should you throw in anything extra to impress the judges just a little bit more? No. If you look around a bit, you'll find former scholarship winners sharing "secrets" about how they won their money by jazzing up their applications with photocopies of their awards, extra essays, or a really adorable picture of their cat. Throwing in extra items that weren't requested *could* be considered innovative and enterprising by certain committees, but do you really want to take that risk? If you include unsolicited documents with your application the judges MIGHT say: "What's with this mess of pages? We never asked for five pounds worth of additional information! This kid obviously can't follow directions, so toss that application straight onto the reject pile."

But if you follow directions and include only what was requested the judges will NEVER say: "Hmm, this applicant only submitted the things that we asked her to provide. Not very creative, is she? We don't want to give this scholarship to a person who does as she's told. Forget that!"

3. Looks Are Everything!

You may be the best applicant of the bunch, but the judges won't know what an outstanding person you are if the information on your application is illegible. It's always best to type your application, but if you must print on the page, do so neatly and in **BLACK INK.**

If the application is made available to be completed online, print a copy first and write out all your answers on it before you fill out the actual form you will send. This may seem time consuming and unnecessary, but it will give you a chance to reflect more carefully on your answers and reduce the risk of making an error on an application you can't get back to correct.

This should go without saying, but if any kind of tragedy befalls one of your pages, for example, a wrinkle, spaghetti sauce, baby slobber, or whatever, it's time to re-write the information onto one of your extra photocopies. Don't wipe your paper with your sleeve and hope the judges won't notice!

4. Complete the Entire Application.

Do not leave any lines blank! If a question does not apply to you, note that on the application, using a full, explanatory sentence, not just "N/A." The best way to have your application rejected right out of the gate is to submit one that is incomplete. Answer everything you are asked and be sure to provide all additional supporting materials requested, such as transcripts, letters of recommendation, essays, etc.

If there are specific eligibility requirements for the scholarship, take extra care to include documentation and thoroughly answer any question that will prove you are qualified to apply.

5. Present a Neat and Organized Packet.

Using staples with application papers is sometimes frowned upon, so, unless instructed otherwise, your best option is to simply paper-clip your materials together before inserting them into your envelope. Avoid confusion by placing the pages in exactly the same order as they were requested.

It is very important that you put your name, Social Security number, and phone number on all pages of the application. Even if your packet is bound together, the pieces can still get detached and/or lost. You don't want some other lucky applicant accidentally getting the credit for YOUR awesome achievements!

Keep your pages pretty and crease-free by using a large envelope that does not require you to fold your application materials.

6. Give Your Application a Final Look Over.

Proofread your entire application carefully. Keep a special lookout for misspelled words or grammatical errors, because you can't rely on computer software to catch your mistakes if you are writing out your application by hand. Just in case you overlooked a mistake, ask your teachers, friends, or parents to proofread it as well.

7. Watch Your Deadlines.

In all my years of applying for scholarships, I have yet to come across a sponsor that has given an extension. If you can't get your application in on time, you definitely will not win! To keep yourself safely on track, impose your own submission date that is at least two weeks before the official deadline. Use the buffer time to make sure everything is included and that your application packet is neat and presentable.

8. Make Sure Your Application Gets Where It Needs to Go.

Before you mail your application, double and triple check that the recipient's address is written correctly. If you are applying for multiple scholarships all at the same time, be EXTREMELY cautious not to slide the wrong packet into the wrong envelope, or you will accomplish nothing beyond confusing two different scholarship committees.

It's a good idea to mail your application using a traceable delivery method, like FedEx, or to pay the small extra fee to request a return receipt. You can rest easy knowing that your application arrived at its destination and was signed for. If you don't receive notice that your envelope was safely delivered, it's time to investigate the situation.

9. Keep a Back-up File in Case Something Goes Wrong.

Didn't get any verification that your scholarship application was delivered? Aren't you glad you made photocopies of everything in the packet before you mailed it? And since you submitted the first application two weeks early, there's plenty of time left for the committee to receive your second attempt!

Also, your photocopies will prove useful if you come across an application similar to another that you've already sent out. You can "cheat" off your own work by copying the answers you gave the time before!

10. Ask For Help If You Need It.

Don't be shy about asking for help with your application. At the very least, you will probably need to work with your parents to collect all the information and documents that must be included in your packet. If you have any questions about the application, do not hesitate to call the funding organization to ask for clarification.

11. I Know I Said Only 10 Tips, But This One is the Most Important.

Remember this is your only chance to show the scholarship committee what an amazing person you are, so don't sell yourself short! My favorite quote is from Benjamin Franklin: "The only thing more expensive than education is ignorance." The most expensive mistake you can make is to ignore the possibility of going to college for free, just because it requires a little leg work. A good education is an investment in your life and it will also affect future generations for years to come.

Easy Ways to Personalize Your Application

In the next few sections, I'll be discussing some individual components of your scholarship application in more detail. Aside from your essay, letters of recommendation, or other inclusions that each individual committee may request, the forms themselves can be limiting in the ways they allow you to express yourself. That said, I will tell you just a couple of ways to make your application stand out from the crowd.

Be Specific, If There's Room

It is standard procedure for scholarship applications to ask you to list your achievements, community service, and awards. Sometimes a simple "list" is all that you can fit into the space provided, but if there IS some extra room, it is always a good idea to expand upon each item and point out the significance of the achievement. This practice is called annotation, which Webster's dictionary defines as "a note added by way of comment or explanation." At the end of this book, you will find an *annotated* appendix of resources for online scholarship searches. Rather than simply listing relevant website addresses, I have also included further helpful details and my impressions of each site. This is what you should strive to do when reporting your activities and accomplishments (though on a much smaller scale). If you write down that you won a "Hostess Award" you may leave the scholarship committee wondering, "Just how many snack cakes did the girl have to eat to win *that?*" Instead, tell them "Winner of Hostess Award, given to the female student most dedicated to easing the transition process of new students entering our school system."

More examples:

NO – Volunteer at local animal shelter.

YES – I believe that every living creature deserves proper care and a place to belong, so I volunteer for ten hours per week at Furry Friends No-Kill Shelter, where I help abused and abandoned animals find loving and committed adoptive families.

NO – Hobbies: Skateboarding and Sudoku

YES – I enjoy skateboarding because the sport keeps my body healthy, my reactions lightning quick, and also provides fun challenges as I learn new skills and tricks. To exercise my mind, I like to complete Sudoku books and try to beat my own speed record with every puzzle.

The more specific you can be about what you do and why, the better the judges will get to know you as a person. It may prove worthwhile to create a master list of your annotated scholastic achievements, awards, clubs and activities, community service work, etc., which you can use as a guide when filling out paperwork. Some scholarship applications do not provide lines for you to record these items, but instead ask you to submit your own list on a separate sheet of paper. Yours will already be ready—score!

Adjust Your Application for Different Organizations

If you can make some calls or do some other simple research, it will always work to your advantage if you know a little bit about the individual or organization that is awarding the scholarship money. One way to use this information is to adapt your preliminary application so that your accomplishments best match up with the sponsor's cause or beliefs. You can arrange the order of your list to highlight the activities the organization is most likely to value, or simply focus more attention on those aspects of your resume that pertain to the sponsor's own agenda. Your application packet can be tailored in many ways to fit with a specific type of scholarship, and we will talk more about how to do this in upcoming sections.

Never Enough Money:
Ionnie's Scholarship Story

If there was one thing that Ionnie McNeill learned a lot about while growing up, it was money.

When Ionnie was only seven years old, her mother began sharing the world of finance with her young daughter through investment meetings and finance clubs for kids. "I was exposed to investing so early on that I couldn't really say whether I liked or didn't like it," Ionnie said. "I didn't know what I liked yet."

As things turned out, not only did Ionnie like investing, she grew to LOVE it! She began building her stock portfolio while still in elementary school, and by middle school she had followed in her entrepreneur mothe"s footsteps and started her own business teaching other children about investing. At age 12, Ionnie was the keynote speaker at the Building Wealth Conference in New York City, and "The Baby Billionaire," as she calls herself, has continued to accept nationwide public speaking engagements ever since.

By high school, there was no doubt that Ionnie was a girl who was going places. So it's no surprise that winning the top $10,000 prize in Guardian Insurance's "Girls Going Places" competition became the first of her many scholarship successes. But winning scholarships wasn't as easy for Ionnie as sitting back and watching her stock profits steadily rise. "The biggest challenge that I faced was not being awarded many of the scholarships that I initially applied for, because I did not meet the financial need requirement," Ionnie said.

Yes, Ionnie had more monetary assets than many high school students did, but she knew that her financial resources would not stretch far enough to cover the tuition costs of graduating from her dream school, Howard University in Washington DC. Serious scholarship winnings were necessary if Ionnie wished to achieve her educational goals, and before she was through, the determined young lady had collected $100,750 in awards.

"You cannot win anything if you don't apply. The most important part of life is just showing up. Therefore, the more applications you complete and submit, the better your chances are at winning."

While doggedly pursuing scholarships, Ionnie stayed organized and on top of the game by creating individual folders for each scholarship she applied for. She treated the applications as if they were assigned homework, making it a priority to complete and submit each one on time.

Now working toward a master's degree in accounting, Ionnie most appreciates the fringe benefits that accompanied her scholarship winnings: "... most of the major scholarships that I won gave me national recognition for my entrepreneurship endeavors. So, not only did they help pay for school, but I also used them to market my business."

Notes

_____

_____

_____

_____

_____

_____

_____

_____

_____

_____

_____

_____

_____

_____

_____

_____

_____

_____

_____

_____

_____

_____

_____

_____

Notes

Chapter Four
Write a Freakin' Awesome Essay!

I can already hear you saying, "An essay? Are you serious? Have you forgotten about my straight C-average in English class?"

Yes, I have to agree with you. I've already mentioned that I loved writing in high school, but one of the few exceptions to my hobby was the dreaded scholarship essay...the gut-wrenching, time-consuming, ball-busting scholarship essay. It sucks. Writing can be fun when it's on your own terms, but in an essay application you can easily get nailed with a topic that's too stupid, too hard, or just way too booorrriiinnngg. Usually, the question will be something about you, and who wants to talk about themselves? It's almost guaranteed that writer's block is going to slap you in the face over and over again until you're dizzy! And on top of all that comes the incredible pressure! You *know* that you aren't just writing for your own pleasure. You *know* that your written words are the ticket to your future college funding, and if you screw up this essay, it could mean curtains for your career dreams. The pressure to succeed is intimidating enough to make your fingers tremble above your laptop keys.

On that note, here's my advice:

Suck it up and quit whining! Instead of fearing the required essay, you should embrace it. Even if you don't think you're any good at writing, creative essay composition is still an area where a C-student can flourish. This is your chance to stand out and be noticed! And, trust me when I say you're going to need it. If you can't impress the scholarship committee with your collection of awards and high GPA, your next best bet is to WOW them with a super-spectacular essay!

You may be proudly smug to write on your scholarship application that you were elected president of your drama club, but keep in mind that there are approximately 27,468 high schools in the United States (and this number includes only *public* schools). Every school has a drama club, and every drama club has a president—chances are you won't be the only applicant to show up with dramatic distinction!

Long lists of volunteer work and extracurricular activities can be impressive, but they all read very much the same. Words written onto blank lines don't tell much about the person behind the accomplishments, and these statistics can even be misleading. Do you really want to go head-to-head with Shirley Perkins, who belongs to sixteen different school clubs, if the scholarship award is based on application alone? Don't you want the chance to expose Shirley for the fraud that she is? Maybe you only volunteered for one non-profit organization, but you poured your heart and soul into the cause. Shirley padded her application by showing up for only ONE day of work with twenty organizations she didn't especially care about! Let's see *her* write about her achievements with even a small iota of passion.

The scholarship essay is your best friend because it's your only chance to rise above your mediocre GPA, your pathetic SAT score, and the fact that most of your "volunteer work" involved babysitting your little stepbrother and then finding out that Dad considers providing you with room and board payment enough to cover your lost time. Complete your essay carefully and thoughtfully, and you just might show up those Honor Society geniuses who were foolish enough to compete with your creativity!

Why an Essay?

A scholarship application does not always require an essay. Sometimes the unique element that distinguishes competitors from one another is something more specific to the sponsor's purpose. For instance, The Gallery Collection, a company that produces holiday cards, holds an annual "Create-A-Greeting-Card $10,000 Scholarship Contest." To enter, all an applicant is required to do is submit some basic information and an original design for the front of a greeting card. A scholarship awarded to future green scientists might ask that each hopeful recipient conduct and document a project related to environmental conservation. You get the point.

In the majority of cases, the sponsoring organization wants to learn more about you through a written essay. Why is this? You might be tempted to answer, "Because it's quick and easy, duh!" Not so much. It takes time and energy for a panel of judges to read and evaluate a few thousand essays, even if they are 500 words or less! The real answer is that scholarship sponsors, whether from academic institutions or simply your local Lions Club, understand that communication is important. Wherever your life happens to meander, you will encounter numerous situations where the ability to clearly express your ideas, desires and expectations can save your butt! Clear, concise writing may easily be the key to your future success in life.

"Forget that!" you might say. "I'm going to be a physical therapist; I'll never need to write." Not true. Everybody writes! You plan to go to college, don't you? Do you think your scholarship essay will be the last one you're asked to compose? Of course not, but let's take a look beyond your college application essay, your assignments for English 101 and, potentially, your graduate dissertation. Will you ever need to communicate through writing in real life? Unless you suddenly fall into a coma, the answer is yes. You were probably right when you complained to your Algebra teacher that you would NEVER have a reason to solve a trigonometric equation once you left her class, but using words to accomplish your goals is a process that occurs on a day-to-day basis. A physical therapist, for example, may need to type up a list of instructions to explain what his patient needs to do at home to care for a dislocated kneecap. If the benched football player gets confused by your unclear writing and makes his injury worse, it could be curtains for his team that season and no business for you the next season when the same athlete tears a tendon.

Even an agoraphobic living in his grandma's basement, who never talks face-to-face with anyone, can benefit from well-honed essay writing skills. He might purchase a piece of unstable software through an online vender that crashes his whole computer system. Once the man's PC is up and running again, he will probably want to ask for a refund. Do you think the company will respond to an e-mail reading, "You suck. I want my money back!"? Not likely. The unfortunate loner is more apt to have his Paypal account credited if he presents his argument more effectively, by using the same structure and style you will find in a scholarship essay:

- Introduction = I'm not satisfied with the quality of your product.

- Thesis Statement = I want a refund.

- Body = List of examples and evidence of why the product doesn't work.

- Conclusion = Here is the action I will take if you refuse to refund my money.

Even if you never win a scholarship and even if you give up on your dream of attending college, an ability to communicate effectively with others will serve you well in life. Scholarship committees and educators know this, which is why the essay has become such a staple of academic learning. Just think of the revolution we could have in the area of male/female relationships if all men were practiced at expressing their thoughts and feelings, and if all women could learn to stay on topic and get to the point!

Okay, enough about the future. Developing good writing skills will benefit you on life's journey. Blah, blah, blah. Sure it will, but you need to produce a winning essay RIGHT NOW to collect your share of scholarship awards! Let's see if I can help.

Before You Write...

Okay, you've found a bunch of scholarships you feel qualified to win, your applications are filled out and stacked in a neat pile with the first due on the top, you've got manila envelopes and a sheet of stamps waiting patiently in your desk drawer, but you can proceed no further without tackling the most nerve-wracking and time-consuming obstacle—the scholarship essays.

I'm not promising to make your essay spew forth from your heart and soul like Jolly Rancher candies from a broken piñata, but I hope I can alleviate the pain just a little with the following tips and tricks:

Work Hard, But Don't Do Extra Work!

Many coaching materials for writing a winning scholarship essay advise you to prep yourself by first compiling lists of your achievements, hobbies, special attributes, and anything else that might make for a riveting essay topic. They even suggest that you write a few practice essays to get into the spirit of the effort. This is very wise advice, because as the cliché that you never should use in your scholarship essay goes, "Practice makes perfect."

Innovative planning is great if it's the summer between your freshman and sophomore years and you're sitting at home bored because all your friends are away at band camp. In this case, sure, make those Excel spreadsheets of your accomplishments and study *The Elements of Style*. The distraction will keep you from obsessing over the advantage everyone else will have when completing scholarship applications because they went to music camp, while you stayed home singing along with oldies on the radio.

My prediction is that it's too late for you to waste time starting at the very beginning of potential essay planning. My guess is that you are reading this book mid-way through your senior year, you've got several specific essay questions sitting in front of you (one with a submission deadline just two weeks away), and you are ready to GO! It's okay that you've waited until now to explore ideas on how to ensure that your essay is a money-maker. It's easier to be prepared if you know exactly what you need to be prepared *for*. So, jump right in! Consider Old Mrs. Johnson's freshmen writing class as your "practice," and be grateful for the enthusiasm she used when applying her red correction pen to your papers. You've got a collection of scholarship essay assignments already, so you can ignore any instruction that doesn't apply to your situation and focus solely on the task at hand—writing a brilliant essay that fits the needs for your most current scholarship competition. You may even have an advantage over the people who started worrying about their writing before they ever looked at a scholarship application. While you are casually perusing a website listing and saying, "Sweet, here's an essay topic that truly interests me," the others may be desperately scouring the databases as they moan, "I wrote an awesome essay about my views on global warming while I was practicing last year! Why aren't any of the scholarship committees asking *that* question?"

Ponder the Question

I hope you haven't waited *too* long, and you've left yourself at least a little bit of time to reflect upon your essay topic. It is often very helpful to mull ideas over in your mind for a few days before committing to write your scholarship essay on the first answer that popped into your head after reading the question. If you are a typical teenager, it stands to reason that your immediate thoughts on any given subject are very similar to what everybody else your age is thinking. You can attribute a desire to be just like your friends to the Collective Unconscious, or blame it on MTV, but the point is that even if you strive to dress like every other teenager in America, use the same social networking tools as every other teenager in America, and mouth off to your parents like every other teenager in America, when you present yourself to the scholarship judges you DO NOT want to sound the same as everybody else. We'll talk more about finding your creative edge later on in the chapter, but the first step is to calmly consider your essay's theme from every possible angle. You might be hit with a burst of inspirational genius, which will allow you to skip the next few sections of this book. E-mailing me to ask for a refund on the unread pages will get you nowhere, but go ahead and try. The writing practice will do you good.

What Will I Be Forced to Write About?

Lose the attitude, will you? Nobody's forcing you to do anything! (And if someone *is*, that person is torturing you purely out of love.) The bottom line is that the scholarship committees are offering you FREE MONEY, so you should cut them some slack and cheerfully write those essays no matter how "pointless" or "hard" you think their selected topics may be. If you win some scholarships, graduate from college, and become rich and successful, then YOU can give away your own award money and pose whatever essay questions you want!

Here are some general groupings for the most common questions poised in scholarship essay writing competitions:

Questions about you as an individual—Scholarship committees want to know why they should award their money to you above everyone else, so it's quite natural for them to ask for more details about who you really are. These types of essays may inquire about areas of your life such as your personal achievements, experiences, influences, goals for the future, background, or financial situation. Some examples of "you" essay topics are:

- ❍ Tell us about a time when you proved yourself to be an exceptional leader.

- ❍ What would you most like to accomplish over the next ten years?

- ❍ In what way has your racial heritage influenced the person you are today?

- ❍ What advice would you give to high school students who are concerned about financing their future college education?

Questions about the organization's primary interest—Some scholarship sponsors are affiliated with a specific group or mission. In many cases, a scholarship essay will be assigned on a topic that relates to an organization's specialty, which comes as no surprise. For instance, it's completely logical to assume, even before you've read the rules, that science fiction author L. Ron Hubbard's ongoing "Writers of the Future Contest" requires applicants to submit a work of fantasy or sci-fi! Some examples of organization-specific essay questions are:

○ How has the American Miniature Horse affected your life? (The AMHA)

○ Write an essay on Lincoln and the Mexican-American War. (Lincoln Forum)

○ Write an essay on why hunting is important to you and/ or your family? (National Wild Turkey Federation)

○ Write an essay about the separation of church and state, and why this is important to our country. (Freedom from Religion Foundation)

Questions about your career choice—Many scholarships are given to young people who plan to pursue a particular field of study. For these awards, the essay question often asks the applicants WHAT drew them to that specific career, HOW they plan to achieve their long-term goals in the chosen field, or WHY they think they have what it takes to succeed as a professional (fill in the blank). Some examples of career choice questions are:

○ How will education advance your plans for a career in law enforcement?

○ What qualities do you possess that will make you a good animal trainer?

○ How do you intend to benefit your community with your training?

○ At what age did you decide to become an entomologist and why?

Questions about our world in general—Frequently, scholarship essay questions will focus on commonly shared experiences such as current events or social issues. The sponsoring organization may have a vested interest in politics, environmental causes, or humanitarian efforts. Alternatively, the committee may simply want to see what applicants can do with an intelligent and thought-provoking topic. Essay questions of this type can be very specific, or they may ask something broader like, "What is the one thing you would most like to change about the world?" Some examples of worldview questions are:

- How could America's economic policies be changed to help working families?

- If you were a famous movie star, which charity would you choose to support with your abundant wealth?

- How will your life change if our country exhausts its supply of oil?

- If you had ten minutes with the president to talk about America's health care crisis, what would you tell him?

Questions about something unfathomable—Some essay topics are thrown out seemingly at random. The question may not seem to address anything of real importance, but before you decide that the scholarship committee was being lazy or whimsical, take a closer look to see if you can detect some subtle, underlying purpose or intention. No? Okay, now here's your chance to embrace the challenge of revealing your special achievements and personality while sticking to a topic that doesn't relate to you in any outwardly observable way. Some examples of totally bizarre questions are:

- If you could bring one animal back from the brink of extinction, which animal would it be and why?

- Write an essay about the wildest party you ever attended.

- If you were only allowed to keep ten of your current possessions, which ones would you chose?

- If you had to emigrate, which country would you choose to live in and why?

- How much wood do YOU think a woodchuck would chuck if a woodchuck could chuck wood?

- Do you believe that Elvis Presley is still alive?

Telling Your Story in the Context of Your Topic

The assigned topic for your scholarship essay might be very specific, or the committee may have given you miles of leeway to choose something personal to write about. Whatever the topic appears to be on the surface, the essay is really about YOU. When you are asked to share your views on global warming, or sum up in 500 words or less why apples are more nutritious than donuts, the underlying question is always "Why do you deserve to win our scholarship?" Many sponsors simply forgo the theatrics and ask that question upfront. Whenever you brainstorm ideas for a new essay, Rule #1 will always be: Reveal Something of Yourself in Everything That You Write. Naturally, you are the best person to write about yourself, because nobody knows you better than YOU!

The scholarship committee wants you to tell your story, because they are looking for a reason to decide that YOU are the type of person who has the qualities they deem worthy of recognition. They want to feel certain that YOU deserve the chance they are offering above and beyond other potential recipients who may have applied. In order for them to see beyond the mere words you've typed on a page, and into your heart and mind, you'll have to present something of your true self to the judges through your response to their chosen essay topic. In about 90 percent of cases, this act is exceedingly easy to accomplish because the committee chooses a question that intentionally provides you with ample opportunity to "tell them a little bit about yourself." Go back to the previous section and read the twenty randomly selected example essay topics. How many of them include the word "you?"

Obviously, if you are asked to describe your thoughts and emotions on the morning of 9/11, you will have trouble avoiding a personal revelation, but what if the essay topic doesn't involve you at all?

"I have to write 1,000 words on Harriet Tubman and the Underground Railroad," you might say. "How can the essay possibly be about *me?*" It IS about you, because you are the one telling the story, so you are the one sharing your reactions and opinions on the subject. Find some aspect of the topic that is meaningful to you, and let the judges see your passion. Heavily researching the life of Harriet Tubman until you know every available fact about her is only the right tactic if you are auditioning for the position of Underground Railroad Expert on a television game show. Unless your grandpa happens to have Harriet's personal diary hidden in his basement, you won't know anything about the woman that your competitors aren't able to learn themselves through a simple online search. Even in the rare case of recovering a long-lost diary, you'll be better off relating her journal-keeping to your own blog than focusing solely on the life of Mrs. Tubman. Better yet, describe your relationship with your grandfather and explain why he may have faked a copy of a historical document (Harriet Tubman could not read or write).

I've stressed over and over that the judges MUST see glimpses of you in the contents of your essay, but don't go getting a swollen head. It's not *all* about you, ego-maniac. Depending on the question asked, or the length of your essay, a small glimpse may be all that you can afford to give of yourself. Fortunately, what makes up "you" is more than just your actual traits and achievements. "You" are also your family, your friends, and your community, so don't be afraid to share claim in the experiences of others when their hardships or triumphs have influenced your own view of the world. Even when not speaking directly about yourself, your choice of words and the importance you place on specific facts or events can say a lot about you as a person.

Five Guidelines for Finding Your Voice

1. Be Original—Originality is the prime directive when writing scholarship essays, because it's essential that your work stands out from the crowd. You may think it's impossible to come up with a truly unique idea amongst hundreds of other applicants all answering the same query, but you've got a secret weapon at your disposal. If you need a hint, refer to Rule #1. Right, the secret weapon is YOU. The words in the assigned topic or question may be the same for everyone, but your own experiences with the subject matter is what will differentiate your answer from all the others. Examine the question and find the best way to relate the subject to your own life, even if the topic seems utterly foreign to your daily existence. If you are asked to write an essay focusing on the malaria epidemic in Africa, you may find yourself growing frustrated as you wonder how you can reveal personal information about yourself when you've never suffered from malaria and you've never visited Africa. Before you begin sobbing in despair, remind yourself that your competitors more than likely share the same disadvantage. It's up to you to find a creative and insightful way to approach any given topic.

The best way to keep your essay original is to avoid the obvious answer. Naturally, malaria is a bad thing, and, of course, this deadly disease should be eradicated from the continent completely. The judges will be reading many, many essays that point out the frightening facts and statistics surrounding this illness and then go on to outline ideas for managing the epidemic. Don't be just another parrot repeating the same research. But don't think that I'm telling you to do the *exact* opposite of what everybody else is doing. It would be a serious mistake to title your essay: "Malaria: Mother Nature's Gift to an Overpopulated World," even if you are the only applicant to submit a paper with that theme!

The toughest part of your essay may easily be generating that first spark of a creative idea to build upon, but I know you can do it! Once you've found the perfect angle of originality, the rest of the writing process should be all downhill.

2. Be Passionate—It takes a lot of spirit to convince somebody that you are the best out of the bunch, but if you can sell yourself, it will mean college money in your pocket! The judges want to know that you are the type of person with the enthusiasm and dedication to take full advantage of your opportunity to be educated. People who care strongly about something are the people who set goals and work hard to achieve them. That's why you have to barrel into your essay with guns blazing! I don't mean that literally. Please, don't hurt anybody.

Most essay questions are open enough to allow applicants to write about the one thing they truly love. Remember Rule #1, and make sure to select a theme for your essay that will allow you to speak with energy and conviction. You may not think the question asked of you has anything to do with your one true devotion in life, but you'd be surprised at how easy it is to relate one subject to another when you add a large dose of passion into the mix.

If you feel backed into a corner, and find yourself unable to work up any enthusiasm for the essay topic, it's time to explore and seek out the hidden passion you may be harboring for that subject. "My assignment is to describe the best muffin I've ever eaten," you say. "I like muffins okay, but I just can't get excited over them." Are you sure? Sounds like the perfect excuse to go on a muffin-eating spree! Forget your low-fat diet for a few minutes, and try out some new flavors and brands. In your frenzy, you may find the world's most delectable muffin, and discover a passion for breakfast foods that will have the scholarship judges quickly signing you a check before they rush out to the nearest bakery!

3. Be Honest—Don't try to fake it. Put your best effort into finding an original and passionate approach to the essay topic, one that will allow you to present yourself in an honest and positive way. Lying about or exaggerating your accomplishments to give the judges what you think they want to hear will work against you. They are smart people, and they will know if your essay sounds forced.

At the same time, don't undersell yourself and your achievements. Honesty works both ways; it's just as much of a lie to conceal your true self out of a sense of modesty as it is to make up events that never happened.

One thing to guard against is the temptation to base your essay on unrealistic goals, no matter how much you'd love to be able to achieve them. Don't tell the judges that you want to become a medical scientist and discover a cure for leukemia. You are not going to guilt them into thinking that by not awarding the scholarship to you they are essentially sentencing thousands of future children to terminal illness. The committee knows that scientists have spent decades searching for a leukemia cure, and you are not likely to sweep in and solve the problem singlehandedly. There's nothing wrong with dreaming big, but compose your essay around *achievable* steps you'd like to take toward the prevention and treatment of disease. Be honest about your passions, but keep it realistic.

Apply everything you've learned so far, and realize that if your essay is not original and about YOU, it is dishonest. If you have no passion for your subject, it's also dishonest. Using complete honesty while writing your essay will help you stick to the tactics and principles that make for a winner!

4. Be Descriptive—Nothing will start a classroom full of preschoolers picking their noses and pulling each other's hair faster than their teacher reading a boring book out loud. Nobody likes a boring story, so make sure that *your* story keeps those judges riveted and awed. "My life is sort of boring," you might be tempted to say, "and their question is even *more* boring!" Yes, that's somewhat true—real life seldom includes high-speed car chases and saving innocent puppies from hoards of rotting zombies. The one way you can help the mundane sound a little more exciting is by using descriptive writing. Lift your words so high from the page that they slap the judges in the face! I'm sure you've heard a teacher or two mention the phrase, "Show, don't tell." Whatever idea you are trying to sell to the scholarship committee, they need to be able to touch, taste, see, smell, and feel your story and why it is special to you.

This is a perfectly decent sentence:

"When I visited a pueblo in rural Mexico, I felt sad because the town was so dirty and the people looked so poor."

Yes, the sentence above is acceptable. It neatly sums up an emotional moment in a person's life, but while the sentence tells a story, it doesn't tell *enough* to make the reader experience what this author felt when she encountered real poverty for the very first time.

○ How was the town dirty?

○ What was it that made the people look poor?

○ How did the author's "sadness" actually feel?

Here is a better effort toward "showing" the reader what life was really like in that poverty-stricken village:

"When I visited a rural area of Mexico, I wandered through the dusty pueblo, carefully avoiding piles of rotting garbage that littered the street. The pungent odor filling my nostrils, and with each hot intake of breath was a mixture of animal dung and dried mud, but it was also the stench of abject poverty. A small child approached me on scrawny, stick legs protruding from underneath a dress so dirty and tattered that I could barely discern its original color. She smiled up at me sadly, her palm outstretched in the universal sign language of "I'm hungry; please feed me." I wanted to give the girl a friendly "Hola!" along with the coins that I dropped into her hand, but the word caught in my throat as my eyes welled up with tears."

You probably agree that the second example is an improvement over the first, but I'm sure you also noticed that the description is much, much longer. "I'm only allowed to use 500 words!" I hear you wailing.

Okay, fine. Sometimes you must sacrifice vivid description for the sake of brevity, but that's still no excuse for boring, vague sentences.

Try this one:

"When I visited a pueblo in rural Mexico, I felt like crying because the garbage-strewn town was so dirty and the ragged, undernourished people were very poor."

Is that better?

Remember that a little bit of sensory description can turn the drab into the dramatic, but go easy on those adjectives. Because one will generally do the trick, there is no need to bury your meaning beneath flowery language. You only get 500 words, you know.

5. Be Positive—Attending college is all about optimism for the future. Your scholarship essay should be upbeat and confident, just like your intentions for your career and the rest of your life. Don't try to impress the judges with your caustic, jaded view of the world. Criticizing society for its stupidity might generate appreciation for your blog, but the scholarship committee doesn't want to be responsible for setting your negativity loose upon the educational world.

The judges also hate reading "tear-jerkers" with no salvation in sight. A sad story is almost as bad as a boring story, especially if the sad story is about *your* life. Your essay is not about making people feel so sorry for you that they wouldn't be able to sleep at night if they *didn't* give you a scholarship. This tactic doesn't work on the judges.

Positivity is the key, but it doesn't mean your essay should be perky (please, please don't make it perky). Conflict and strong emotion are essential parts of good story telling. It's absolutely okay to write about the hardships that you've overcome in your life, just don't forget the oh-so-important "overcoming" part! A triumphant conclusion is what changes a tear jerker into an award-winning literary masterpiece. Your essay shouldn't be in denial about the sorrows that plague our world, but it also can't dwell on the futility of attempts to move forward. In the earlier example of the girl who visited Mexico, her heart-wrenching essay presumably ends on a positive note, as she explains her plan to improve at least a small part of the harsh world that she witnessed. The scholarship sponsors want to educate people who are hopeful for change and willing to work hard to achieve it, not those who are starting out pessimistic and defeated.

Knowing When to Shut Up

Don't Be Smart—Needing to buy this book means, you've already established yourself as a less-than-spectacular student. Don't try to trick the judges into thinking you're a genius in disguise by bombarding them with big words and complicated themes. There is a far greater chance of them laughing at the incomprehensible mess of words on your paper than declaring you a prodigy and putting you straight on a bus to Harvard. There are plenty of scholarship essays out there specifically designed to test the applicant's higher intelligence, but your GPA has already rendered you ineligible to compete in such battles of cerebral superiority. Give up the charade of scholarly academia and just be your creative, resourceful, C-earning self.

Don't confuse fake intellect with genuine insight. If you think of a new and interesting way to look at a subject, go with it! Don't let the brainiacs out there intercept your brilliant observation, because they'll only fumble and drop it. If something you want to say feels smart, dont hesitate to type it up. You'll know if your vocabulary or insights are forced.

Don't Be Stupid—There are many ways to bomb your essay with stupid content, especially when you are scrambling for a creative edge. Remember, you want to portray yourself as a person who will succeed in a college environment. Despite all the movies that make dorm life seem like one big party, you won't win a scholarship with an essay that begins: "I deserve to go to college because I can hold my alcohol better than anybody else I know." Even if it seems like an honest and original approach, avoid any essay topics that will define you as a slacker or, worse yet, a criminal. Now, I'm not trying to dissuade you from writing about the things that you find most pleasurable in life. If your passion is online gaming, I'm sure you can come up with an intellectual analogy to relate *World of Warcraft* to the struggle of America's first settlers, but I wouldn't recommend writing an essay that describes your ideal afternoon as one spent sprawled on the couch while you bitch-slap prostitutes in *Grand Theft Auto*.

Humor is another pitfall of potential stupidity. Telling a joke or two is a great way to ease the judges into feeling comfortable with you. If you can raise a chuckle, your essay will definitely be remembered! But, before you insert humor, carefully consider the appropriateness of your joke. The same wisecracks that make your friends laugh until they squirt milk out of their nostrils probably won't be equally appreciated by a 45-year-old scholarship judge. Too much frivolity and the judges won't take your essay very seriously, but if you offend them with a joke that is in poor taste, your entire application could wind up in the trash. Before you add a touch of humor, ask yourself these three questions:

○ "Could I tell this joke to my grandmother?"

○ "Is this joke truly funny, or is it just silly?"

○ "Could this joke be considered offensive?"

When gauging the possible reaction to your humor, it's important to consider your audience. You probably won't know who exactly is judging any given scholarship competition, but it's a safe guess that they'll be around the same age as your parents—and you know how humorless those people can get! Another clue you can use is the type of organization that is sponsoring the award. For example, I told a joke at the beginning of this chapter that played off the stereotype that women are too talkative. While this kind of humor is appropriate (and even tame) for a readership of high school students, it wouldn't go over very well in a scholarship essay written for the Feminist Majority Foundation!

You can probably think of even more misguided essay mistakes than I've listed here, so use that insight to avoid writing something that will make the judges' eyebrows shoot up in disbelief at your audacity. If you can't trust your own judgment when determining the appropriateness of a topic or a joke, test the idea out on your (most sensible) friends and family members.

Don't Be Repetitive—When writing your essay, assume that the scholarship committee has already read over your application. Don't just repeat the things about yourself that you've already told them, because that's the kind of time-waster that will make the judges yawn and set your essay aside without ever giving it a second thought. This is the time to hit those judges with something interesting and new!

Know the Organization

This trick doesn't work in every situation, but sometimes researching the sponsoring group, institution, or individual can go a long way toward helping you settle on the perfect essay topic. If the organization has a specific purpose or interest, it is wise to compose an essay that aligns with these goals, or, at least, not in direct opposition!

I'm not telling you to become a brown-nosing suck-up, or to pretend that the sponsor's mission is the most important thing in the world to you when you've actually never heard of a charity dedicated to the betterment of pond frogs living in urban environments. Think back to Rule #1 (Five Guidelines for Finding Your Voice) and remind yourself that this essay is about YOU. Before all else, you must stay true to yourself and write honestly about your own passions. However, this does not mean that you should wreck your chances of winning by submitting an essay that will make these particular judges grind their teeth in annoyance. Learn more about the organization, and if you absolutely do not agree with their views, wad up the application and toss it in the trash. Faking it is never a good idea.

In most cases, you will easily be able to find some common ground between your own interests and the cause the scholarship sponsor values the most. Practice choosing essay titles that will impress specific organizations by taking the short quiz below.

1. The scholarship is being sponsored by *The Humanist—A Magazine of Critical Inquiry and Social Concern.* Which of the following is the best title for your essay:

   a. The Rights of Americans—the Ones They Don't Tell You You've Lost

   b. What I've Learned From My Dog

   c. My Goals For the Next Ten Years

2. The Catholic Church where your grandmother worships is offering a scholarship to a worthy teen who wishes to attend a religion-based institution of higher learning. They require applicants to submit an essay expressing their views on abortion. Which of the following is the *least* appropriate title for this essay:

   a. The Adoption Alternative

   b. God Believes That Every Child Deserves a Chance

   c. Free Will Includes Freedom of Choice for Women

3. A scholarship is being given away by a local hardware store, but only first-generation children of immigrants are eligible to apply. Which of these is the most effective title for your essay:

   a. How I Spent My Summer Vacation

   b. Dad Gets Arrested: A Story of Prejudice in America

   c. Is War Ever the Answer?

Your Plan of Attack

You've taken all my advice to heart, and now you've come up with a brilliant essay topic that is original, passionate, appropriate, and, most importantly, presents YOU as the world's most excellent candidate for a scholarship award! But, before you begin enthusiastically pounding on your keyboard, you may want to take some time to flesh out your thoughts and devise your plan for sharing this phenomenal idea with the scholarship committee.

Every essay, no matter how long or short it is, needs to have a distinct beginning, middle, and end. Somewhere during your school career, you probably learned how to create an outline to guide you through the composition of a research paper, short story, or even a book report. If you have the main components of your essay organized in some meaningful way before you sit down to actually commit it to paper, you may find yourself less frustrated and susceptible to hair-tearing mental blocks. Your organization method could be a formally constructed outline, a piece of scratch paper covered in a scrawl of brainstorming, or maybe you've got everything stored in neat compartments inside your head. However you choose to accomplish it, the important thing is having a soft, cushiony plan to land on before you leap headfirst into the task of writing.

Set up Your Workspace

Before you embark upon your essay writing journey, make sure that you've prepared a comfortable setting for this often uncomfortable assignment. Gather in advance any equipment or research materials you may need and choose a working location with the right atmosphere to relax you and facilitate your creative success. You know where you do your best work, and I don't mean where you do the most work, because if you're anything like me, that will be in homeroom, at the last minute before the bell rings to announce your first period class! We're talking about where you work BEST.

Maybe you write best when sitting outside under a tree, surrounded by the sounds and smells of nature. If you don't like stopping to brush bugs off your laptop screen, you might prefer locking yourself in the privacy of your bedroom with a "Do Not Disturb Under Penalty of Death," sign taped to your door. You may be a person who needs complete silence to think, or maybe you find it impossible to concentrate without heavy metal music pounding your ear drums. If you are most comfortable lying on your back, take the old-school approach and write your first draft in a notebook with a well-sharpened pencil. Surrounding yourself with fragrance and bubbles while writing in the bathtub may be your favorite way to get your creative juices flowing, but if your laptop doesn't have a strong battery, I suggest that you try out that pencil and notepad combo. As far as I know, there aren't any good scholarships offered for victims of electrocution.

If you are striving to produce a successful essay, set yourself up for success from the very beginning by removing all distractions and creating a writing environment that is ideal for YOU. If you need your brothers and sisters relocated to a different country in order for this to happen, I'm sure your parents will understand. After all, they've been claiming for years that nothing is more important than your education, right?

Don't Give Up Now!

You've got your essay question in front of you, your desktop is neatly tidied, the house is empty and quiet, and the cursor is blinking happily at the beginning of a fresh Word document. Your computer screen glows with optimism, the creative possibilities are endless, but you've got nothing. Your mind is as blank as your newly-created page.

No matter how much advice you've been given on how to write a winning scholarship essay, it's often extremely hard to come up with a good idea and begin the process of committing your thoughts to paper. But if you are tempted to say "Screw it," and just give up, remind yourself that you might be sacrificing a scholarship you would have won to that evil demon called writer's block.

There was a scholarship that I almost didn't apply for, solely because the essay topic was too hard. The money was offered by the League of Women Voters organization, and they were asking applicants to answer the question:

"What Am I Doing to Make Democracy Work?"

My initial reaction was, "What??? I'm only seventeen years old—I don't know!"

I pondered the question for a few days, and then tried again to formulate an essay idea, but it just wasn't happening. My baffled mind kept screaming, "I don't know anything about democracy! I can't even remember the words to the Pledge of Allegiance most mornings!"

A few days more, and my only new thought on the subject was, "I go to history class. Does that count? What else do you possibly expect a teenager to do?" At this point, I decided the best thing might be to spare my brain further agony and just give up. I didn't even know what the word democracy really meant, so how could I write anything intelligent about a subject that so obviously had nothing to do with the life of the average teen? It occurred to me that maybe I ought to at least know the *definition* of democracy before I wrote it off as a concept that was completely incomprehensible, so I picked up the family dictionary and flipped to the d-listings. There, just beneath the word "demobilize," I read:

"a : Government by the people; *especially* rule of the majority b : a government in which the supreme power is vested in the people and exercised by them directly or indirectly through a system of representation usually involving periodically held free elections..."

See? My confusion was justified. What was I supposed to know about elected governments when I wasn't even old enough to vote yet?!

Still, the words of that definition stuck with me, constantly nagging at the back of my mind: "... power is vested in the people and exercised by them directly or indirectly through a system of representation..." Finally, it hit me. I was a part of democracy in action after all! At that time, I volunteered in my local Youth Court, where I helped to prosecute and defend other teenagers who had committed minor crimes and were lucky enough to avoid the fate of a more formal court hearing. This job was exactly like what the dictionary said about democracy, because "we, the people" had "power vested" in us to decide the punishments of our peers by "directly exercising" our authority through a system of representation. Okay, maybe that was a bit of a stretch, but nobody can deny that the U.S. judicial system is a crucial branch of our democratic government. And I took part in making that system work, even though I was "only" a kid!

This realization convinced me to plunge ahead and write the essay I'd come so close to blowing off. Recalling my time spent in the courtroom, I was literally able to start my essay off with a bang of the gavel, of course. I'm so glad that I overcame my fear of the topic, because not only did I win the scholarship, but that interview was also one of the most interesting sessions that I ever attended!

All right, you probably are thinking, "Good for you, but whoop-de-do. How am I supposed to get past my writer's block?" Okay, fine, if my success story was not inspiring enough for you, here are five writer's block-busting tips to get you started on that oh-so-frustrating essay:

1. **Remember that this is your first draft, and relax a little.** You are probably feeling crushed by the heavy importance of this assignment. This essay isn't about the difference between a C or a C-minus on your report card, it could win you hundreds of dollars! Yeah, that's a lot of pressure for a kid to handle. But, here's the deal: A member of the scholarship committee is not standing next to your printer ready to snatch the essay pages away the second they are spit out. If this first draft kind of sucks, then so what? Anything you write now can work as a basis for the really sweet, absolutely perfect essay you will eventually include in your application packet.

2. **If you need to get your motor warmed up, start by writing something else.** Did you learn any fun writing exercises in your high school English classes? If not, think of anything else you could write just to get the feel for putting words onto a page. Maybe spring break is almost here, and you can warm up by typing out a set of instructions for your neighbor on how to take care of the pets while your family is away on vacation. Just about any type of writing will work, as long as you

keep it simple. If you start composing an angry letter to your mean boss at Pizza Hut, the emotions involved in the project might put you in the wrong state of mind for moving on to more positive writing.

3. **Don't start at the beginning. If it's the opening of your essay that's got you stumped, skip that part for now.** You know what you want to say in some of the other sections, so write those parts down, even if the end result is a series of stand-alone sentences. You'll get your thoughts linked before you know it!

4. **Force yourself to write. If none of my other suggestions have jump-started your flow of creativity yet, set a timer for fifteen minutes and just force those fingers to tap on the keyboard.** Often simply doing it can spark a real interest that will carry you away on a wave of productivity. But, if not, at least you tried. Delete the crap you wrote today, but know that your valiant attempt will only increase your likelihood of getting things done "for real" tomorrow!

5. **Do it later. Sometimes even the most prolific writers are totally not in the mood to concentrate on their work.** Sure, you might have been planning all week to spend the hours of 2 p.m.–5 p.m. on Sunday writing your killer scholarship essay, but if your girlfriend dumps you that morning, your ability to focus on anything else will be as good as dead. Or, maybe you just got some exciting news that's kept you grinning uncontrollably for hours. You may be feeling too boisterous and full of anticipation to settle down and take your essay seriously. Channel that optimism, if you can, but don't push it. Sometimes the time just ain't right to write!

While You Are Writing...

Bow to the Whim of the Powers That Be

Yes, you are original and creative! You are a free spirit—a rebel who doesn't take orders from anybody... right?

Wrong! You *do* take orders from people who want to give you money. Don't just skim the instructions for writing your scholarship essay. Read them CAREFULLY and OBEY THEM. Remember in kindergarten when you got a smiley face sticker as a reward for following directions? Well, you're grown up now, and the prize this time is the gigantic check the scholarship committee hands to you. But your essay won't pass inspection unless you submit it *exactly* as requested. The topic may be comprised of several parts, so you must be sure to address each aspect as it was asked. Here is an example of a multi-part essay question, taken from a $1,000 scholarship sponsored by Communities and Schools:

"Discuss the top three priorities in your life and indicate why you made these your priorities."

The committee is essentially asking you for six pieces of information: three priorities, plus three reasons why. In this case, I answered each of the six queries within the text of my essay, and I walked away with the scholarship. If I had only discussed my two top priorities, I doubt I would have won, no matter how well my essay was written!

Some scholarship essays or projects come with few instructions or guidelines, but whatever the committee asks for, give them precisely that. If they ask for a 1,000-word essay, don't write 819 words or 1,333. If they ask for two pages, double-spaced, don't give them 1.5 spacing so you'll have more room to write. If they ask you to submit your essay written in purple ink on the back of a cobra skin, get out your brightest marker and your snake-hunting stick. You may have written a beautiful poem about the ugliness of true love, but don't turn it in as a substitute for the essay on nuclear disarmament that the application requires. Follow the instructions. If kindergarteners can do it, so can you!

What's the Point?

By the time you sit down to write, you've probably already decided what message you hope you get across to the essay judges. Yes, the underlying theme is always "Give me the money, because I'm the best," but there will also be some more direct point you need to make before you print out your finished document. Your essay's main idea is typically referred to as your thesis. If you've never heard this term before, put down my book and go look it up. Now!

Once you've written the perfect thesis statement for your essay, you need to stick to it! Make sure that each point or idea within the body of your paper clearly relates back to the primary overall concept you've established in the beginning. Don't let your words go wandering off on irrelevant tangents. Trust me; you won't be able to confuse the judges into awarding you their scholarship.

Go in With a Bang!

Sometimes it's a good idea to save the best for last, but not when you write your scholarship essay! Don't leave the judges plodding along hoping that your writing will pick up its pace somewhere before the end. Get out those metaphorical guns I mentioned before, and start them blazing right from the beginning! If you think it's a good idea to begin your essay by stating, "*Hi, my name is Felecia, and I deserve to win this scholarship because…*" you may as well give up right now and find your nearest military recruiting station. Your name, rank, and serial number will be easier to recite in monotone than your scholastic statistics.

I realize that the parameters of an essay's structure can limit your ability to get *too* creative, but you can always find a way to catch your reader's attention right from the start. One method, which I used in my scholarship-winning essay titled, "My Fabulous Future in Television Production," was mentioning some aspect of life that nearly everyone can relate to:

"As a child sitting in front of the television, you never really think about how that cartoon or TV show you're watching came about. Furthermore, you are completely unaware of the hard work it takes to bring that show together. The only thing that matters to you is entertainment."

When people are reminded of some universal experience, like being an oblivious child engrossed by the antics of Bugs Bunny, they will nod to themselves as they think, "She's right. I never did understand where my cartoons came from!" Now, you have a friend, because you've both shared the same fond memory.

A little bit of dialogue will enliven any story, and it's especially effective at drawing in your readers when the essay opens with some exclamation:

"Sammy, get down from there right now!" My mother called up to where I stood unsteadily on the roof of our house.

"Sure, Mom," I piped back, in my squeaky six-year-old voice. I opened an umbrella, and in an awkward imitation of Mary Poppins, leapt right into my very first emergency room trip. The umbrella experiment was an utter failure, but there in the hospital, with both arms plastered in fresh casts, I resolved that I would someday feel the thrill of a free fall ending in a successful landing. Now, with my recently earned skydiver's license in my wallet, I can say with conviction that you should never give up on your dreams.

A third way to make your opening (or your entire essay) interesting, is to use a relatable aspect of life to create an analogy that illustrates your main idea. Here is an example opening from another of my scholarship winning essays, where I compare the priorities in my life to positions of importance in a vehicle headed down the road of life:

"Although I treat everything in my life with the utmost importance, here are three things that stand out above the rest. First of all, my education is in the driver's seat, with a seat belt on. The priority riding in the passenger seat is the set of positive relationships I make with people along the road of life.

My third priority—the passengers in the backseat—is community service and my other extra-curricular activities. As I drive toward success, a combination of the three will enable me to live a prosperous life."

Another attention-getting opening gambit is to throw an interesting quote into the mix. For instance:

According to legend, famous circus owner, P. T. Barnum, once said: "You can fool some of the people all of the time; you can fool all of the people some of the time, but you can never fool all of the people all of the time." I know that **ALL** of you judges will be reading this essay, so I won't try to fool your group into thinking I'm some great academic. My strengths and my passions lie in other areas of life, and I hope you will agree with me that certain non-scholarly accomplishments can be even more important than a high GPA."

I'll leave it up to you to devise your own scheme for catching the attention of the judges, but keep in mind that the first impression you give them will set the tone for the rest of your essay.

Write Like a Winner!

Sorry, but I've got bad news for you—I can't teach you how to write well in just a few paragraphs. The good news is that you'll find no end to the resources available to assist you with comma placement, verb tenses, and other important aspects of English composition. I'll give you a list of things to remember while writing your essay; if you don't understand a writing rule mentioned here visit your local library to check out a book on the subject, or consult the Grammar Girl **website: http://www.grammar. quickanddirtytips.com**

I can't advise you against every dangling participle or explain each gerund clause in the English language, but here are a few tips for making your essay a winner:

- ○ Use proper punctuation.
- ○ Write tight, clear sentences.
- ○ Vary your sentence structure.
- ○ Use active voice, not passive voice.
- ○ Avoid fragments and run-on sentences.

○ Make sure that your nouns and your verbs are in agreement.

○ Be careful about altering verb tenses accidentally.

○ Transition smoothly from one paragraph to the next.

○ Finally, know the precise meaning of a word before you use it in your essay!

Leave With a Bang!

Okay, cock those guns again and get to banging. You already know you want to lure those judges into caring about your essay with an exciting opening, but you also need to leave them with something to remember. The conclusion of your essay is the last part they'll read, so it will be the freshest thing on their minds when they reflect upon each applicant.

Your conclusion does exactly what the name claims—it closes your essay and brings your message to a big finish. This is a good place to remind your audience of your main idea, but DON'T overdo it! No matter what you may have been taught in freshman composition class, nobody needs to hear you summarize all of the points in your essay. The paper wasn't that long; I think they can remember. You know that feeling of elation you experience as you exit the theater after seeing a movie where good has triumphed over evil? Do you think the blockbuster would leave you with the same sense of satisfaction if the hero turned to his companion at the end and said, *"Over the course of our adventures, we have located the magical arrow, defeated the evil king, and rescued the captive princess. Now, we are free to ride away into the sunset triumphantly…until the sequel, when the Dark Lord shall rise again to be vanquished by us for a second time."* This isn't good storytelling. Remember that your scholarship essay is YOUR story, so tell it in a way that makes people listen in rapt attention, not roll their eyes and say, "Do you think we're stupid? You already told us that!"

If you feel the need to summarize your essay in the conclusion, at least present the information in a whole new way. Get out your thesaurus and look up a few synonyms. But please promise me that you will never, ever announce to your readers that your essay is about to end by beginning your final paragraph with "In conclusion…" or "To summarize…" They know it's over. They can see that the words are about to stop.

"Fine," you say, "You've told me what not to do, now how 'bout sharing a few tips on the way I SHOULD conclude my essay?"

Your conclusion should definitely link back to your beginning, bringing the essay full circle, but you want to avoid simply repeating your introduction. Remember my example of Sammy, the incompetent six-year-old skydiver? Let's say that his essay is answering the question, "Tell us about a goal you've already set and conquered in your life, and explain the process of your success." Sam might begin his conclusion by saying:

On the day of my very first sky dive, Mom was waiting on the ground with her cell phone in her hand, her finger poised to dial 9-1-1. I was proud of myself when I proved to her that all enthusiastic leaps of passion do not have to end in pain and disaster. As I complete my education, I will always look back on my skydiving lessons to remind myself that even the wildest, most reckless dreams can be made a reality if I am persistent and dedicated to achieving my goal.

I can't tell you *exactly* how you should conclude your essay, because the topics and formats vary drastically from scholarship to scholarship. Your best bet is to determine what information the committee wants from you, and make sure you've given it to them, but here are some common questions you might ask yourself as you compose your conclusion:

- ○ What have I learned?

- ○ How can I use this knowledge?

- ○ What are my future goals?

- ○ Why are they important?

- ○ What is my next step?

- ○ How can I encourage my audience to put further thought into my subject?

To illustrate my points, take a look at this introduction to an essay written by a girl who longs to save the endangered orca whale population of the Salish Sea:

While riding in my father's boat as we navigate the passages between the San Juan Islands, I am tempted to lean against the deck railing, chin in hand, while I think to myself, "Boring!" But, I don't. While the wide expanse of dark water surrounding me all looks very much the same, my eyes are alert and my interest is piqued. At any moment, I might hear a wet exhale of air and see the upward jet of water that indicates the nearby presence of an orca whale! The times in my life when I've been lucky enough to witness a pod of these majestic animals feeding or at play are my most treasured memories. I'm dedicated to my goal of becoming an environmental scientist and discovering new ways to protect marine life from extinction, because I cannot imagine living in a world where the unique possibility of encountering a wild orca whale no longer exists.

Would this be an interesting and effective way to for the girl to conclude her essay?

In summary, the orca whale population of the Salish Sea is being threatened by pollution, food shortages, and too few females of breeding age who can add calves to the pod. To help fight these threats, I have volunteered for many beach clean-up projects, written letters to my senator asking for the removal of the dams that are killing the salmon, and campaigned for the release and rehabilitation of an adult female who was captured from these waters many years ago. As I finish school to become an environmental scientist, I will continue to do everything that I can to help these whales that I love.

Not so great? I agree. The girl has merely repeated what we can assume she already told the judges in the body of her essay. Let's give her a second try at catching her audience's attention:

As I ponder these things, a young male orca surfaces only a few yards away from Dad's boat. He breaches joyfully before my eyes, and I consider the splash of water that hits my face when he lands to be the whale's thank you for all my attempts to help his

pod—both past and future. The orca's beauty and grace heighten my resolve to become an environmental scientist, so that I can work toward finding solutions for marine mammals at risk of extinction. If the top predators of our oceans can't be saved, what hope does that leave for the top predators on land—mankind?

Much better, isn't it? Using exactly the same number of words as she did before, the girl has written a new conclusion that is more than just a litany of her essay's previous content. She has linked back to her introduction by returning to the boat scene where she began. Without boring her audience by repeating the details, she has reminded them of her two main points: a) the orcas are going extinct; b) she has been active in trying to stop this from happening. She has stated her intention to continue to fight for the environment, and she's told her readers why her goal is of importance to them by posing a question they may never have considered before. That's a lot to accomplish in only four sentences, but I know YOU can do the same, if you put some thought and attention into writing your conclusion.

Tantalizing Titles

Isn't the title supposed to come first? Why have I waited until the end of the section to mention them? I've left the first part of your essay for last, because it often makes sense for you to wait until you've completed your writing to decide on a title.

Your title should accomplish two things. First and foremost, it must tell the judges what your essay is about. The next step is to be sure that your title is interesting enough to catch the judges' attention.

Let's say you've been asked the question, "Why do you want to go to college?"

The WORST title choice you can make is "Why I Want to Go to College," (unless, of course, the instructions specifically tell you to use that as your title—always follow directions).

Before you pick a title, think about how you intend to approach the question. This is why it's okay to wait until you're done writing before titling your essay, because then you'll *know* how you approached the question!

If you are going to talk about how much you will enjoy attending college, you might title your essay, "My Education: An Exciting Adventure About to Begin."

If you want to tell the judges about your dream to graduate from clown college so you can spend your life distracting rodeo bulls, you might choose "Laughing in the Face of Danger," as your title.

If you are the first in your family to attempt college, "Ambassador to Higher Education," might be a good title.

You Get the Point

"What if the essay instructions don't tell me I need a title?" I hear you whine. Well, do they say you *shouldn't* have one? How can a title possibly hurt? Your essay is a work of art, and what great work of art ever goes untitled? Have you ever read a book called, *A Book*? Have you ever gone to the theater to watch *A Movie*? Do you have a dream of one day going to Paris to see that statue with no arms that they've got on display in the Louvre?

'Nuff said.

After You've Written...

Your essay is not complete just because you've typed the last word and hit "Save." There are more steps you need to take before you seal and mail your scholarship application. They are the three "RE's" to RE-member: Rewrite, Recheck, and Reuse.

Rewrite

The first draft of your essay is, well, your first draft. Before you go bragging to Mom about your masterpiece, read it over and see if you find places where your point could be clearer or where your prose could use some general improvement. A good way to tell how well the words of your essay flow is to read it out loud to yourself. If you stumble over an awkward sentence, you'll know exactly what needs a bit of fixing.

It goes without saying, but along with your grammar and punctuation, you should take a second look at your spelling. In this age of computer software, there is no excuse for overlooking misspelled words, but you still must keep an eye out for misplaced homonyms that your spell check program cannot detect. You don't want your essay to read: "When the village chieftain served me the *meet*, I *new their* was something amiss, because the animal's *feat* were *steel* moving!"

Also, the rewriting stage is an ideal time to rethink some of your content and get rid of any stupid puns like, "They are the three "RE's to RE-member." You want to sound like a future college student, not Dr. Seuss!

Recheck

When you are confident that your essay is ready to be viewed by the general public, it's a good idea to have several people read it over to offer suggestions and point out errors. And, no, this is not cheating. You are a resourceful "C" student who knows how to get things done in the quickest and most efficient way! Learning is all about knowing where to find information that you need, if it's not already in your head. When you get to college, there won't be any rules about who's allowed to proofread your essay. If the scholarship committee wanted to test your ability to write without research or assistance, they would lock you in an empty room with a piece of paper and a surprise essay topic.

The trick to getting help, however, is to find someone knowledgeable and reliable to read over your essay. I'm not saying that you shouldn't show it to Mom, but she is probably too biased to give you constructive feedback. Remember how proudly she tacked that picture you drew up on the wall, even though it looked more like a deformed hippopotamus than the horse you meant it to be? Also, your little brother is not a good choice for a proofreader, even if you can get him to do it just by threatening to delete his Facebook account. A good, reliable critic could be an educated neighbor or extended family member, but one of your teachers is also an excellent choice. Your English instructor will probably be more enthusiastic about helping you than your shop teacher or gym coach, but you never know.

If you think it's worth the investment, you can get your essay edited and critiqued by one of approximately 8,000 writing services on the Internet. The more you are willing to pay, the quicker you will have your results in your hand. One of these services, PaperCheck.com, holds an essay competition twice each year for a $500 prize. This leads me to wonder how many essays their editors have critiqued only to have the new drafts submitted to their contest!

You can also hire someone to write your essay for you, but this is a very bad idea. Not only will your purchased essay fail to tell the judges anything about YOU, but there is also a monster that hunts down and eats people who cheat in scholarship competitions. You've been warned.

Reuse

If you can make it work, it's perfectly acceptable to tweak one of your essays for submission to multiple scholarship contests. No matter how much agony they put you through during the writing process, never rip up your essays or delte the files. You never know when a good essay on "How the Internet Has Changed My Grandmother's Life," might come in handy later.

One excellent way to get more mileage out of old scholarship essays is to adapt them for submission in college application packets. Acceptance committees often use the same questions or topics you've encountered during your scholarship search. All socially conscious students should recycle!

Play the Essay Critiquing Game!

Here's your chance to practice your essay-flaw detection skills by critiquing the following pair of examples:

A fictional organization, the 42nd Street Herpetological Society, is offering a $1,000 scholarship to a worthy high school student who has an interest in reptile ownership. The essay question requirements are as follows:

"Tell us in a paragraph of ten sentences or less why you think snakes make good pets."

Ted submits his essay well before the deadline, but he doesn't invest much time in the composition. Read over Ted's essay and see how many errors in style and adherence to the question you can recognize:

Why Snakes Make Good Pets

(1) Lots of people keep snakes as pets and there are many good reasons why. **(2)** Snakes are very quiet, and small ones don't take up very much space. **(3)** They don't need to be taken outside several times each day. **(4)** These are qualities that make snakes good pets for apartment-dwellers. **(5)** Snakes don't eat very often, so you can go away for the weekend and you won't have to find someone to feed your pet while you are gone. **(6)** Since they don't eat very much, they also don't often poop. **(7)** This means less clean-up than you get with other types of pets. **(8)** Reptiles are known for their long lifespans, so you will have your pet for many years. **(9)** But snakes can also be expensive because they need fancy tanks, and in some cities you must pay a lot of money for a license to own one. **(10)** Scorpions and tarantulas also make good pets for all of the same reasons as snakes. **(11)** Lots of cool people own snakes, like celebrities and rock stars.

Did you spot any problems?

Ted's essay is informative and his writing mechanics are good enough, but he broke many of the rules of good scholarship essay writing:

- ○ Ted's title is merely a repeat of the assigned question.

- ○ He doesn't excite the judges with his bland and simple introduction.

- ○ He gives reasons why snakes make BAD pets, which is the opposite of what the committee wants to hear.

- ○ Ted goes off topic when he starts talking about arachnids.

- ○ He offers no real conclusion to his essay.

- ○ He broke the rules by writing eleven sentences.

- ○ Worst of all, the essay is boring and Ted shows no passion for his subject.

Sarah writes a much more passionate essay about keeping a snake as a pet. After beginning with a creative title, she resists the urge to simply list the many attributes of a snake. Instead, she shares a slice of herself by telling a personal story. However, Sarah's essay is overrun with mechanical errors. Try proofreading the essay to see if you can detect them all:

My beloved Bailey: better than a dog

(1) When I was six years old my family had a picnic down by the pond and a snake slithered out of the grass right next to our blanket. **(2)** My mother screamed, but for me it was love at first site. **(3)** The reptile was so beautiful. **(4)** Because its scales were iridescent. **(5)** After that experience, it became my goal to own a majestic and u-neek snake as a pet. **(6)** I finally convinced my parents to buy me a Boa Constrictor for my 10th birthday. **(7)** My dad understood how a snake would work out well in our apartment because they are quiet they are low-maintenance, too. **(8)** Mom was skeptical at first; but I won her over by reminding her that a snake doesn't shed on the furniture like a dog would. **(9)** I named my boa "Bailey," and she's been my loyal friend for the past eight years. **(10)** I haven't never had another pet as interesting, clean, or easy to take care of as Bailey the boa!

Answers:

○ All the title words (except "a") should be capitalized.

○ Sentence #1 would benefit from a couple of commas.

○ In sentence #2, "site" is used in place of its homophone "sight."

○ Sentence #4 is a fragment.

- ❍ In sentence #5, the word "unique," is spelled incorrectly.

- ❍ In sentence #6, boa constrictor should not be capitalized.

- ❍ Sentence #7 is a run-on.

- ❍ Sentence #8 should have a comma in place of the semi-colon.

- ❍ Sentence #10 is a grammatical nightmare.

Two Samples of Winning Essays

I've included a couple of the essays that helped me win my scholarships: the essay on democracy that I talked about earlier and a sample of an essay about my favorite type of community service work.

Question: "What Am I Doing to Make Democracy Work?"

My response:

The Right to be Tried by a Jury of Your Peers

BANG!

The gavel fell, and the judge announced, "I hereby sentence you to clean the graffiti off the store building, and to put in 30 volunteer hours assisting with the community youth center's afterschool arts and crafts program."

The defendant groaned and rolled his eyes, but I could see his clenched muscles relax in relief. My own face was outwardly stern and professional, but inside I was grinning like crazy. Although I had just finished prosecuting this defendant for vandalism, I couldn't help but admire the unique masterpieces that he spray-painted illegally on the sides of private buildings around our city. The teenager needed to realize that there are consequences for a person's actions, but I was glad to see him given an opportunity to put his artistic skills to good use, rather than being punished with a useless fine or time spent in a juvenile detention facility with the more hardened young criminals of our community. That is what my job is all about—exercising my freedom as an American to help our judicial system productively help the people it serves. This is why I feel that my participation in Youth Court enhances my responsibility in making democracy work.

In a healthy democracy, citizens have the information and skills to participate effectively in society. The Youth Court is a Juvenile Assessment Program that focuses on teaching young people their rights, and showing teenage offenders that in order for them to make an easier transition to adulthood they must be held accountable for their actions.

I am a volunteer for my local Youth Court, and through this program we strive to bring out the best in American democracy through proven strategies in civic education, family involvement, and community volunteerism. We volunteers serve in a real courtroom setting, taking on the responsibilities of prosecution and defense attorneys, clerks, or bailiffs. Using this hands-on method, we arbitrate crimes committed by young offenders and develop their mistakes into lifelong learning experiences. Working together with one another to resolve problems for the common good is the key to healthy communities and stronger nations.

As participants in this program, the other volunteers and I are constantly applauded for our commitment in studying the issues placed before us and acting upon our opinions. With the help of local judges and attorneys, we have become politically educated, and have gained a better understanding of how government works and how we can make our voices heard. This knowledge has helped motivate us to get involved with helping other young people to learn about their own responsibilities within their community. As active youth, "We Are the People" and the future of this nation. Through my volunteer work with Youth Court and the influence I have had on my peers, I feel that I have contributed toward making democracy work—one case at a time.

Question: "Describe a particular aspect of your service activities and accomplishments and relate the impact it has had on you and those you served."

My response:

A Brighter Future for Mariah…and for Me!

"Good job, Mariah! All the answers on your multiplication worksheet are correct," I congratulated my honorary "little sister." The 10-year-old beamed up at me, so I went on to say, "You're so good at math. Have you ever thought about becoming an engineer or a scientist?"

"I dunno," Mariah replied.

"So, what do you think you want to be when you grow up?"

The little girl just shrugged, and I realized that she had probably never been asked this oh-so-common question before. As a student mentor, I've encountered so many children who don't have attentive adults in their lives to initiate these kinds of conversations. Nobody has ever told these kids that they should strive for excellence and they can do anything that they put their minds to. That's the part I play in being a mentor.

The ability to volunteer within one's own community is a skill possessed by only a handful of people. I believe the trait that makes my character shine is my willingness to help others. Through my experiences volunteering, my eyes have been opened to a world that is unfair, where bad things happen to very undeserving people. I spend a lot of my time doing things in the community, but I am most dedicated to being a student mentor to younger children who need attention and encouragement. My time spent with Mariah has been full of enrichment, as I show her a world outside of her own.

I met Mariah last year at a summer camp for underprivileged youth. After that first encounter the two of us were inseparable. Mariah is the second youngest of five children, and I know from personal experience that it's sometimes hard to get the attention you yearn for from your parents, even though I come from a family of four, not seven! I guess that's why we connected so well; I understood where she was coming from in her need for attention. I started spending the majority of my days with Mariah, but now that school is back in session, our friendship is limited to tutoring, weekend visits, and long phone conversations.

Looking back at the time I've spent with Mariah, I have seen her evolve into a happier and more industrious child. John Ruskin once said, "Give a little love to a child and you get a great deal back." That's the part of the work that benefits me, because I have never had someone like a little sister who looked up to me. The impact this experience has had on me is irreplaceable and has instilled in me a new love of the world and what it has to offer. It has also taught me responsibility. I know I have had a dramatic impact on Mariah's life, as well. For example, her name is no longer on the Disciplinary List at school, but instead on the Honor Roll, plus her once heart-breaking facial expressions have transformed into sunshine-filled smiles and belly-aching laughter. Someday, we may even discover together what it is she wants to be when she grows up!

Awarded For Essays:
Mckenzie's Scholarship Story

Mckenzie began his senior year confident that he would be attending college soon after he left high school. His family was far from rich, but his parents believed in the power of education, so they had managed to put aside a moderate college fund for their son's future. Mack's plan was to stretch the money as far as he could by enrolling in a community college, where he could earn a two-year degree and settle on a major before transferring to a larger university.

Everything changed in the spring of that year, only three months before graduation. Mckenzie had a disagreement with his father—the kind that ends with, "If you're going to live in my house, you'll obey my rules!" followed by, "Fine, then I won't live in your house, if that's what you want!"

Mack was getting along fine while living in his car or occasionally staying at a friend's house. Despite his hardships, he made sure to attend school each day and keep up with his class work, so he wouldn't fall behind in his education. Mack's biggest concern was how he would manage to pay for college, now that he was supporting himself on only the meager wages of a job in the fast food industry.

Mckenzie had never considered applying for scholarships, and he knew nothing about the process. He visited his school's career center, but didn't find any offers that looked promising. Mack did take one application—for students hoping to become elementary school teachers, because he figured there wouldn't be much competition. He began working on the required essay, but his heart wasn't in it. Mckenzie came from a long line of teachers, but he wasn't convinced that he wanted to carry on the family tradition.

The scholarship essay was not the only one that Mack had prepared that spring. He was enrolled in a creative writing class, where he was expected to complete essay assignments, along with composing poetry and short stories. Mack's writing was so well appreciated that he was appointed the prose editor position on his high school literary magazine. Later in the year, the creative writing teacher began turning her students' focus toward entering competitions. Whenever she learned of a new youth writing contest, the entire class was required to prepare an entry whether or not they intended to submit their work for the judges to review. Mckenzie was squarely in the "not" category, but he was unaware that his teacher had been mailing entries to competitions on his behalf. That spring, while Mack was living out of his tiny Toyota, the letters of congratulation began pouring in. With each winning submission, Mack was expected to attend another annoying awards banquet. He didn't mind the free food; the problem was being forced to wear a suit and tie! The rear-view mirror of his car was not designed for getting gussied up for a formal event. But no banquet meant no prize (usually just a stupid gift certificate, anyway), so Mckenzie put on the dumb suit—nicely accented by a leather jacket and sneakers—and attended each ceremony.

As the school year was winding to a close, Mack got called into the principal's office.

"We're trying to think of some way to reward you for winning so many writing competitions," the principal told him. "You've made our school look very good."

Money would be nice, Mckenzie thought, but out loud he said, "Thank you."

"We'll be giving you the English Student of the Year award, of course," the principal continued, smiling at him warmly.

"Thank you," Mack replied. Inside he was thinking, *Yeah, the plaque will look great nailed to the bumper of my car.*

"Also, we've decided to give you a complimentary ticket to the Senior Prom."

"Thank you." *Just what I need— another opportunity to wear a tie.*

"And a scholarship spot on the senior field trip."

"Thank you."

Whoopee, a visit to the capital to see democracy in action.

The principal must have sensed how unimpressed Mckenzie was with the list of rewards, so he rummaged around in his desk drawer and withdrew a small, shiny object. "Here, it's a lapel pin with the school's crest on it."

"Thank you." Mack took his pin and left.

Several weeks later, he was again summoned to the principal's office. This time, the news was considerably better.

"I've been told that you wish to enroll in a community college," the man said. "Is this true, Mckenzie?"

"Sure that's the plan."

"Do you care which one?" the principal asked.

"Not particularly."

"There's an opportunity for a full scholarship to the community college across town, if you're interested. Books included."

"Really?" Mack asked. "How do I apply?"

"You don't," the principal told him. "You've already got it. It's up to our school to select a winner, and since you've already written so many excellent essays and stories for us, we've decided to skip the competition and offer it directly to you."

"Thank you!"

All because of his essays and the relationship he built with the higher ups at his school, Mckenzie was able to complete his AA degree while he saved money for his continuing education.

Notes

Notes

Chapter Five
Recommendation Letters That Rock!

In your essay, you're given a quick chance to show the scholarship judges who you are, but they don't generally take your word for it. Just like a man whose doctor tells him he's got only a week to live, the judges want a second opinion. They get this by asking you to provide recommendation letters from people who know you well and can offer the committee a different look at you and your accomplishments.

"Not fair," you might say, "I only want the judges to know the stuff about me that *I* choose to tell them!" Don't sweat it. While it's true that someone else is going to chime in and tell their own little secrets about you, you aren't relinquishing all control of the situation. Letters of recommendation are a GOOD thing, because you get to pick who will represent you before the scholarship committee. I'm sure that you're a fabulous person, and everybody you've met just adores the heck out of you, but there's always *somebody* who has an ever-so-slightly negative opinion about the validity of your charms. (Right, these people are totally just jealous!) The good news is that the judges will never talk to your enemies! This is a scholarship decision, not a parole hearing, so those few people who don't believe in you simply aren't invited to speak. Furthermore, the judges don't have the time or inclination to hunt down any people who don't like you. You don't need to worry that someone on the committee will find out how you ambushed your mailman with a paint bomb when you were twelve, because nobody will sit outside your house waiting to interrogate him behind your back. As long as the juvenile court record is sealed, the secrets of your past are safe.

What is a Letter of Recommendation?

Okay, the answer to that question is obvious. It's a letter from a third party that explains to the scholarship committee why YOU are the best person to receive their offered funding. A more helpful question may be, "What type of information goes into a recommendation letter?" This is a question you should know the answer to because chances are that somebody you ask to write one won't have a clue!

Good recommendation letters are as varied as the people who write them, but to give you an idea of how they can look, let me describe a basic structure that can be followed. This is the type of page that you can actually create and reproduce as a hand-out to give the individuals you ask to write your letters of recommendation:

Letter of Recommendation – A Basic Format

Salutation

Paragraph #1 – Introduce yourself and explain your relationship to me. How do we know each other, for how long, etc.

Paragraph #2 – Describe your feelings about me in general. What is it about me that you admire? What are my most impressive characteristics?

Paragraph #3 – Tell them about my dreams for the future, and explain why you think that I have the drive to accomplish these important goals.

Paragraph #4 – What qualities do I possess that make me an ideal candidate to receive this specific scholarship? Why would YOU grant me the scholarship if the decision was yours? (This may be generalized if the letter is intended for multiple applications.)

Closing – Thank the committee for reading your letter and considering the candidate for the scholarship. Final thoughts about why I am a good candidate.

Signature - Include contact information if you feel comfortable allowing the committee to call/e-mail you for further information.

I know that the above outline sounds very conceited on your part, but let's keep a few things in mind:

1. The people you ask to write letters on your behalf should already be "fans." You can go into the process assuming that these adults are, in fact, impressed by you and your accomplishments.

2. In order to promote your full potential during the scholarship application process, you need to put aside humility and take on an attitude of "Of course I deserve this money, because we all know that I am awesome!" If you can't sell yourself to the people who already know and love you, how do you expect to convince a group of strangers just how hard you intend to rock the college world?

3. Many of the people that you ask to recommend you will already know how to write this kind of letter. They won't need you to remind them how much they admire you. (More on this idea later.)

Okay, so exactly who are these people who are dying to sing your praises to the scholarship committees?

Choosing Your Recommenders

Throughout your life, there are many people who have helped you to get where you are today. You've beat the odds already by deciding that college is important to you even if your grades are less than amazing, and the adults surrounding you know this! When it comes time to choose which mentors and role models you want representing you, do it C-student style, and be creative… but not too creative. The scholarship committee will probably not appreciate a letter of recommendation that you claim was written by your dog, even if Patches obviously adores you more than any other creature on the planet. I know that paw print signature at the bottom of the letter is super-cute, but rip it up, anyway, and save such ingenuity for your scholarship essay. Recommendation letters are serious!

Finding the Right Person for the Job

When it's time to collect those scholarship recommendation letters, look around your community and make a list of those adults that have spent the most time with you during the past few years. These people are very likely teachers, employers, activity coaches, volunteer coordinators, and the humorless woman who oversees the detention program at your school (hmm…you might want to leave her OFF the list. Just a suggestion.)

The first rule to keep in mind is that you are looking for people who are not only willing to write nice things about you, but who honestly KNOW a few nice things about you! The closer you are to the people you choose, the easier it will be for them to know what to write, and the easier it will be for you to ask them for letters in the first place.

In my case, my Television Production teacher was happy to write me a simply amazing letter of recommendation for me to include in my application packets. I also asked the officer in charge of the youth court where I volunteered my time and expertise. He wrote me a spectacular letter, which included the hours I had worked and the lives I had touched. If you take a look at your own life, full of various classes and activities, I'm sure you will find that there are many wonderful people you know who are in a position to say great things about you!

Here's one little piece of advice before we continue: Resist the temptation to ask a relative to write you a recommendation letter. It's tacky and it's lazy, not to mention the fact that a letter from a relative won't go very far toward impressing the judges. Of course your mommy thinks you're special. The committee would rather hear from someone who is not under any family obligation to like you! However, there are two situations where it may be appropriate to collect a letter from a relative (other than your parents!):

1. If your family member serves a dual role in your life, such as also being your employer, baseball coach, etc.

2. If your family member is in a position of significance that relates to the specific scholarship you are applying to win. For instance, if the award is being offered to a prospective law student, your aunt

the District Attorney may be the best person to explain why she can picture you as a successful lawyer.

In these circumstances, it is a judgment call as to whether or not you should speak to the person about excluding mention of the family relationship when h/she composes your letter. It would not be a "lie" for your uncle, the coordinator of an after-school program for disadvantaged youth to simply state that he has known you all of your life, and that you have come in after school to tutor the children in his program for the past three years. Your uncle's letter would, of course, focus on the quality of your volunteer work, and not mention how you used to entertain everyone at family get-togethers with your poorly crafted magic act. But it's always better not to omit the fact that your recommender is a relative if you think that the full truth behind your relationship may come out one day!

Special "Extra" Qualities Of Good Recommenders

The following attributes are not required, but may be useful in helping you narrow down which people in your life you will first ask to recommend you:

Is the person articulate? Who on your consideration list is especially good with words? If you frequently work on a volunteer crew that cleans up litter off the local beach, your supervisor from the Parks and Recreation Department would be an excellent person to write a letter about you, except for the fact that English may be his second language and putting thoughts onto paper may not come as easily to him as knowing the best way to help a beached whale. Give preference to the people on your list who are known to write and speak eloquently, but don't despair if you really need a letter of recommendation from a person who is less articulate. A creative person like you can always find a way!

Is the person reliable? Your physics teacher is definitely brilliant, and she just LOVED how you built a working nuclear reactor for the science fair using Play-Doh and a hamster on a wheel. The only trouble is that she has hair like Albert Einstein and she is always walking around in an absent-minded daze. Before requesting a letter of recommendation from her, ask yourself if you are prepared to follow-up frequently—almost obsessively—to make sure she gets the letter written on time!

How long have you known the person? It is often impressive to have a recommendation letter written by someone who has been a part of your life for a very long time. If nothing else, this proves that the individual has known you for years and you haven't done anything yet to make this person hate you! Your ability to remain tolerable for extended periods of time can say a lot about your good nature. Keep in mind, however, that simply knowing a person for many years is not enough to make them a good candidate for letter-writing. The person also needs to have a certain amount of credibility. Your best friend, Bertha, has probably admired and emulated you ever since the first grade, but do you really think the scholarship judges will care about her opinion of your extraordinary skills in amateur body piercing and your expertise at slumber party organization?

How well-suited is the person to recommend you for *this* scholarship? If you are entering an art competition, a few good people to ask for letters would be:

- ○ Your art teacher

- ○ Your curator friend at the museum you regularly visit

- ○ The shopkeeper who has hired you six times to paint his storefront window

If you can match your recommendations to the purpose of the scholarship, for example, your pastor for a religious scholarship, your coach for an athletic scholarship, and so forth, their praises will definitely add credibility to your application packet. Just be cautious about choosing people ONLY because of their title or position. Remember that you want recommendation letters from people who are honestly enthusiastic about you and your goals! Definitely do not cheat by seeking out the endorsement of prominent individuals who don't really know you at all. If you start stalking him during your freshman year, you *might* eventually trick George Lucas into signing the bottom of a letter that recommends you for a film school scholarship, but may The Force be with you when the committee finds out that you don't actually know the guy!

Hedge Your Bets

If the scholarship application asks you to include two letters of recommendation, don't just ask the top two people on your list. Make sure you have a third (and even fourth) back-up waiting in the wings in case one of your other deals falls through. Approach anybody and everybody who has a good relationship with you, and ask them to write you a letter. You can never have too many recommendations, and collecting a whole library of them will allow you to pick and choose the best portrayal of you for each individual scholarship. You may even find yourself pleasantly surprised when your auto mechanics instructor, who is the last person on your list, winds up being the person to provide the most stunning letter of recommendation!

But, what if the scholarship instructions ask people to MAIL in their recommendations? There are quite a few committees who want to receive the letters in this fashion (presumably so the author can be completely honest since you will never see the letter). You'll want to make sure that the judges receive the same number of recommendation letters that they asked for, but that they aren't flooded by extras, right? The trick to dealing with this little snag in your finely spun tapestry of organization is to make sure you approach your recommenders early during the scholarship application process. When you come across a committee who insists upon having your recommendations sent in by the individual authors, you will have already established a relationship with your group of expert letter writers. You will know who can be relied upon to hit the mailbox on time, or who will be open to simply signing a past letter that you've adapted on their behalf and sending it out while you are right there to witness the act. I'll explain more about recycling recommendation letters in just a few minutes.

Working With Your Recommenders

You've decided who to ask about writing your letters of recommendation, but how do you go about making it all happen? Start out by approaching each person with an air of humble gratitude and a flattering eagerness to be represented by the best. If someone you've selected says, "I'm sorry, but I'm too busy," or "Not a chance! I've never really liked you and I've started a petition to keep you out of any and all colleges," be polite and understanding. You can make a voodoo doll and fill it with pins later—after all your scholarship applications are turned in on time. To minimize turn downs, follow these easy guidelines that will help your letter gathering run smoothly:

Make it Easy!

Don't expect the busy adults in your life to bend over backward for you until their poor spines crack! The people you approach for recommendations will appreciate that you took the time and initiative to prepare everything they'll need for the job you are asking them to perform. Their cooperation level and the quality of their letters will reflect this appreciation!

Start Early

Just as with every other aspect of the scholarship application process, it is essential that you not wait until the last minute to ask for the letters of recommendation. The best way to end up with a sloppy, poorly conceived letter is to say to a recommender, "I need this finished by tomorrow night, okay?" In such a situation, you'll be lucky to get even a sloppy letter, instead of a flat-out refusal! Thanks to modern technology, today's adults check their e-mail, update their Facebook pages, while still finding the time to do laundry and dishes. They are busy, busy people, and if you don't give them plenty of time to prepare, it's just not happening. Your emergency is not *their* emergency.

Provide All Information

Don't leave your benefactors scratching their heads and wondering what to write about you. Some, like teachers, for example, will have a ton of recommendation letters under their belts already, and they will probably be able to accept your request and run with it. For others, yours could be the first letter of recommendation that they've ever written. A good strategy to help everyone out is to prepare an information packet to hand over when you ask each recommender to represent you. If you are worried about offending the person with your proactive preparation, open with a statement like, "I have gathered together this information that I hope you find to be a helpful reference while writing my recommendation. Somebody else wanted me to provide these materials for him, so I'm giving them to everybody I ask, just in case." Chances are, your recommenders will be grateful for any assistance that will make the job easier!

Your information packet could include:

☆ A guideline for structuring the letter, like the one I offered earlier

☆ An article from the Web about how to write a good scholarship recommendation

☆ Any forms/instructions from the sponsor on how the letters should be presented

☆ Information about the individual scholarship(s), including the purpose, qualifications, etc.

☆ A sheet that lists out your achievements, awards, and anything else that will look good in a recommendation letter

☆ A resume of your past employment history/volunteer work

☆ A copy of a recommendation letter you've already received from someone

☆ An addressed and stamped envelope, if the letter needs to be mailed separately

Write It for Them

I'm sure you've seen those political ads on TV that end with a beaming senator announcing, "My name is Rob U. Blind, and I approve this message!" What the good senator really means is, "I'm too busy to write up my own campaign promises, but I've hired some very smart people to do it for me. I trust their judgment, so let's have a cheer for making public urination illegal nationwide!"

Sometimes, if a potential recommender is either too busy or too daunted by the task of writing a letter, you may want to offer to write one for them to approve and sign. Okay, all you control freaks out there need to quit drooling, because these types of self-written endorsements should be used sparingly, and only with the explicit authorization of the person who is recommending you. Don't suggest this idea to everyone you approach, because the implications can be insulting and the practice is frowned upon by scholarship committees (like they'd even know!), but always be aware that writing your own letter to be approved and signed by someone else IS an option.

My girls' flag football coach devised this scheme without any prompting. When I asked him for a recommendation he said, "I'll sign a recommendation letter for you, but you'll need to help me write it." He was the coolest guy ever, but super-lazy. Thanks to the coach's abhorrence toward composition, I got a killer chance to write exactly what I wanted to write about myself, plus what he wanted to say about me, including how many touchdowns I scored as the running back/wide receiver. If you are going to compose a recommendation letter on for someone else, fist interview the person and find out which of your good qualities the person admires most.

Remind, Don't Nag

When you negotiate the letter deal with your selection of recommenders, be sure to discuss deadlines and delivery dates. Ask to have the completed paperwork handed to you or mailed out well before the application is due, as this will allow time for unexpected set-backs. And, again, make things easy on these people! They are doing YOU a favor, so repay their kindness by taking on most of the responsibility involved. Do NOT say to your English teacher, "Please deliver the completed letter to my house at exactly 9 p.m. on the evening of the 27th. There is a storm warning for that night, so you may have to hitch your Rottweiler to a sled if you want to make it through the snow drifts." Instead, try an approach that will result in a less hostile and sarcastic recommendation letter, like maybe, "I will come by your classroom before school on the morning of the 28th to pick up the letter, does that work for you?"

You don't want any nasty surprises when it comes time to collect your letters, so it's a good idea to remind your benefactors of your request at appropriate intervals. Avoid sounding like a nag by politely asking something like, "How's that recommendation letter coming along? Is there any more information I can give you that might help you out?" or "Remember that letter I asked you to write? Will you have it ready for me by the 28th, you think, or do you need a little bit more time?" If your people have forgotten all about the letter, which is very possible in these hectic times, they will definitely appreciate a casual reminder!

The Final Steps

It's not over just because you've got a few letters of recommendation clutched triumphantly in your sweaty palm. (Hey, don't wrinkle them!) You'll need more recommendations throughout your immediate life—and lots of them—so here are some tips to ensure your smooth sailing in the future.

Recycle and Reuse

Before your journey is complete, you may have applied for twenty or more scholarships. The easiest plan is to just recycle the letters you've got, and re-use them again and again. Your people won't have a problem with it, because they don't want you coming back every other day and asking for a new recommendation letter!

A really good way to accelerate and catapult your "C" Student Express Pack is to use the same recommendation letters over and over again, but before you hit the Xerox machine, discuss the matter of recycling with each of your recommenders and let them decide what level of reuse they feel comfortable taking part in. The matter is not as simple as asking the person not to date/sign the letter so that you can make photocopies for later. You will be much more successful in winning scholarships if your recommendation letters are personalized for each organization or type of award. Such an act obviously requires a lot of work from your recommenders, however, so if you are expecting some of them to represent you in EVERY application, you may encounter resistance. Candidly discuss the matter with your recommenders to be sure that everyone is aware of your recycling plans and is in agreement about the methods. Here are three systems for "recommendation recycling" that you might propose:

GOOD—Your recommender writes you a generic, undated letter addressed "Dear Scholarship Committee." The letter talks about your awesome-ness in general, but does not mention any specifics about a particular scholarship. Some organizations will not accept letters like this, but if they do, you can print off a new copy, get it signed by the author, and then mail it.

BETTER—Your recommender writes your first letter, and gives you a copy of the digital file. He or she grants permission for you to change the date, salutation, and even some of the contents, to personalize the letter for use with other scholarships. When you finish your adaptations, the person will read over what you've written, and sign the bottom if everything looks good. In a case like this, you may need to ask your recommender for a stack of blank pages bearing his/her letterhead so you are equipped for each new printing.

BEST—If your recommender REALLY loves you, he or she might agree to personally compose a new letter for each scholarship application. You might remind this person that much of the content can remain the same each time; just a few small touches can change a letter from generic to specific and personalized.

Learning how to recycle and reuse recommendation letters will save you a lot of work throughout your upcoming educational experience. You may be able to use revised forms of these first scholarship letters for your college admission applications, to gain employment, or even for the future scholarships you will apply for once you've used up the ones you get now! Just be sure that the author of each letter is always aware of how you are using his/her recommendation. As you progress through life, and your high school guidance counselor's praise no longer holds the same clout, you will already know how to manage your next set of recommendation letters.

Thanking Your Recommenders

Your recommenders have done you a big favor, and they deserve to be rewarded! I'm sure you've already verbally thanked them again and again, but how about something more tangible? If you win a gigantic scholarship with their help, you darn well better take them all out for a nice dinner! But in less extreme circumstances, a sincere note of thanks or a Blockbuster gift card will do the trick. A really fun idea for teachers is to have a Thank-You pizza delivered to their classrooms in middle of the school day. Just wait until those recommendation letters are sent out before you disrupt their lessons!

Properly thanking the people who have gone out of their way to assist you is not only polite, but it also fosters goodwill should you ever need to ask these individuals for further recommendations or favors.

A Sample Letter of Recommendation

This very flattering (and honest!) recommendation letter was written by my high school television production teacher:

To Whom It May Concern:

If you desire enthusiasm, dedication, and diligence, then you cannot overlook Felecia Hatcher's application. In the four years that I have had the privilege to teach Felecia, I have watched her constantly strive to be a superior student. These qualities, combined with her strong sense of leadership, make Felecia an invaluable asset to TV Production.

To begin, Felecia doesn't settle for meeting minimum class requirements. Instead, she goes out of her way to cover additional school and community events to broadcast on our daily show. Felecia sees how this extra effort reflects in a better end result, the show. Her leadership skills are commendable as well. Felecia is currently producing our morning show which places her in charge of her peers. I know the respect that Felecia's peers bestow upon her is a direct result of her ability to communicate positively and to not expect anything of her staff that she wouldn't be willing to do herself.

I am honored to share with you the qualities that make Felecia such an outstanding candidate. I recommend her without reservation, knowing she will only enhance your program.

(Teacher's Signature Here)

Overcoming All Obstacles: Jessenia's Scholarship Story

It was unlikely that college would ever be an option for Jessenia. Nobody in her family before her had sought out an education beyond the twelfth grade, and nobody expected that she would do any better for herself. To make matters worse, Jessenia grew up in her state's foster care system, living with families who were generous enough to share their home with a child in need, but in no financial position to pay for her college education.

Jessenia's troubled childhood prevented her from being able to concentrate on her studies, and she finished her junior year of high school with a "C" average. She realized during her senior year that the only way she would achieve her goals in life would be by earning a college degree, and the only way she could pay for college would be by winning scholarships. Jessenia knew that she would be up against some heavy competition when she began to apply: students who had better grades, hours upon hours of community service, and the full support of their families. But Jessenia overcame the challenge by believing that her vision was bigger than her competition. "I knew that there were scholarships available with committee boards that were willing to read or listen to why I deserved a scholarship I just had to build up the courage to tell my real story and put everything out there and not be afraid of people judging me," she says. "I knew that I had a dream and if someone could hear my journey, they would understand my vision to succeed despite the bumps in the road that caused me to have less than perfect grades."

And Jessenia was right! By the time she graduated from college, she had found sympathetic scholarship board members who awarded her $160,000 in scholarships. They listened ot her and believed in her ability to go out and achieve greatness.

How did she do it without high grades and test scores? Jessenia says: "I worked on my writing skills for my essays, and I marketed myself by being vocal and really honest about my experiences. I wanted to leave the scholarship board knowing that they changed a life and they would not regret giving me this opportunity and I found out that I was exactly the kind of person that they wanted to help."

Despite the personal obstacles that she was required to overcome, Jessenia learned that anything is possible with hard work and research, and that there is no excuse for not seeking assistance in financing a college education.

"Scholarships are available for everything under the sun, ranging from your favorite vacation place to being a specific race," she assures other college hopefuls. "While searching for scholarships, I found out that there were millions of dollars available for students if they were to simply apply and don't get discouraged."

P.S. Jessenia is an amazing blogger and a major advocate for adoptee rights. Please visit her website to find out how you can help.
http://www.yourbloodismyblood.blogspot.com

Notes

_____

_____

_____

_____

_____

_____

_____

_____

_____

_____

_____

_____

_____

_____

_____

_____

_____

_____

_____

_____

_____

_____

_____

Notes

Chapter Six
The Scholarship Express Package

I'm not going to lie to you—scholarship applications are HARD to complete! I still have painful memories of the first one that I ever filled out and sent off. It took me almost a MONTH to collect every bit of information that the scholarship committee wanted me to provide and compile and present it in the order they required for submission.

Lucky for you, I have some good news! As I became an expert at filling out applications, I devised a system that allowed me to submit as many as four to five in a single day! Gradually, and without really knowing it was happening, I created an assembly line for applying for scholarships. I realized that the more scholarships I pursued, the more likely the phone would be to ring with good news, but who wants to spend all of their free time filling out paperwork? For the sake of your sanity, it's almost essential to figure out the most efficient way of getting the job done. And the sooner the better! Therefore, I will share my own personal Scholarship Express Package (SEP) secrets, so that you can skip the learning process I went through and immediately become an application-pumping machine!

It All Began With a Binder

As I started to collect scholarship applications, I knew right away that I would need some sort of system to keep myself organized and on top of the game. Without fully understanding how useful it would eventually become for housing my SEP materials, I designated a huge, three-ring binder as the official storage unit for all of my scholarship paperwork.

My binder served a dual purpose of both function and inspiration. There was a clear holder in the very front that I began referring to as my "Dream Pocket." In it, I placed a colorful brochure from the University of North Florida. I had already received a rejection letter from my top choice, the University of Central Florida, so admission to UNF had become my new aspiration. After all, higher is better, right? Why stay central when I could shoot for the very top of my state! Every time I opened my binder, I saw the UNF brochure and it reminded me of my goal to do whatever it took to get accepted and to find the money I would need to attend.

My magic binder was my best friend, and I honestly believe that this folder is the top thing that helped me earn so much college scholarship money, but I soon discovered that absolute success would require more than merely keeping everything I needed confined to one place. That's when I began creating my spreadsheets.

I had a spreadsheet for everything! There was the one that I used to record my high school course list, both past and present; there was the one where I kept a tally of my community service hours; but the most important one was the spreadsheet that I used to organize information about my scholarship applications.

Whenever I picked up an application for a new competition, the first thing I did was whip out my scholarship deadline spreadsheet and start filling in the blanks. First, of course, I would write the name of the scholarship, the award amount, and the date that the application was due. Next, I checked off if I qualified to apply, or if I *could* qualify at some point before the deadline. Finally, I looked the application over and made reminder notes about anything additional I would need to collect, update, or adapt for the particular scholarship.

Using my awesome SEP, I was able to make Wednesdays my official Scholarship Assembly Day. I would visit my school's career center to hunt for any new scholarship opportunities, take home the applications, compile a packet of the required insertions, stuff it all (neatly) into a manila envelope, slap on a few stamps, and have the whole thing ready to mail out the next morning. With this tedious task behind me, I could relax for the rest of the week and focus on accomplishing even more great things to add to my resume of achievements!

Invest some effort into getting yourself organized right in the beginning, and you will find that you save *tons* of valuable time in the long run!

What Do I Need for My SEP?

Good question! You should begin by gathering the items you will need to keep your assembly line running smoothly. Let's start with the basic materials you will need to either purchase or find around the house. Unless you need to mow your neighbor's lawn to earn the money to buy these things, this list of supplies should be the easiest portion of your SEP to obtain:

- ○ Three-ring binder
- ○ 20 clear sheets
- ○ Folders w/three holes
- ○ Black pens
- ○ Large Manila envelopes (10–20)
- ○ Stamps
- ○ Portable USB flash drive

These next items will also be easy enough to collect. All it takes is a quick trip to your school office, plus a few minutes standing in front of a photocopy machine.

- ○ 3–5 copies of your official transcript
- ○ Copies of your unofficial transcript
- ○ Copies of your SAT/ACT Scores
- ○ Copies of your Federal Student Aid Report

Creating your SEP is starting to get a little harder, but I know you're up to the challenge. Now, you will need to prepare a page (with possible updates) on each of the following subjects:

- ○ Scholarship Deadline Sheet

- ❍ Curriculum resume

- ❍ Job resume

- ❍ Activities/clubs resume

- ❍ Community service resume

The final items you will need are the toughest by far:

Essays

As you already know, almost all scholarship committees will ask you to submit an essay. The questions and topics for each one may vary, but you are counting on at least *some* of them being generic enough that you won't have write a fresh essay for each scholarship application. There are several ways to build your personal essay archive, and you will probably use some combination of the three methods that I've listed below:

1. Prepare yourself in advance by researching the five most common essay questions and composing a brilliant example of each. If luck is on your side, you will encounter numerous opportunities to use and reuse this essay library. I know that I advised against wasting energy and brain power on "practice essays" back in Chapter Four, but I'll repeat that it's a beneficial skill-builder and an incredible time saver if you have started playing the scholarship game early enough to indulge in the luxury of pre-preparation.

2. Gather completed essays from your past school career that can be either used directly or adapted to fit within the guidelines of a scholarship application.

3. Save copies of your scholarship essays as you write them. Keep the pages handy in your SEP binder, ready and waiting when needed.

Letters of Recommendation

Like your essay archive, generic recommendation letters can be prepared in advance, but you can also collect them as you go along. Your SEP should contain at least three different letters that can be quickly copied or adapted to fit your needs.

How Do I Assemble My SEP?

Once you've gathered the contents, your Scholar Express Package will be easy to put together:

1. Start by placing your Scholarship Deadline Sheet in the very front where it is readily accessible and easy to use.

2. Next, create a handy portfolio by sliding a copy of each piece of paperwork inside a clear, protective covering. Display everything, including your essays and recommendation letters. Not only will your binder serve as an impressive showcase for your accomplishments (take it along on scholarship interviews), but it will also be a valuable reference tool as you flip through your options and decide which pages will work best for each new scholarship application.

3. Insert folders into the back of your binder and fill them with photocopies of all your important documents. Some pages, such as school transcripts and SAT scores, will be needed for every application, so make a nice stack of copies to avoid emergency trips to Kinko's. Other items, like essay papers, will be used less frequently as straight copies, but it's still a good idea to keep a few ready to stuff into application packets if you don't need to make any alterations.

4. Store envelopes and stamps in the back pocket of your binder. Be sure to keep yourself adequately stocked with these essential supplies.

5. Your portable USB drive will contain digital copies of your typed documents, such as spreadsheets, essays, and letters of recommendation. It's also a good idea to scan and save unofficial digital versions of your other documents. Find a way to attach this USB drive to your SEP binder, so you will always know where it is when you need it. Be sure that you back-up the contents of your portable drive onto your computer, just in case of disaster!

How Do I Use My SEP?

Ah, finally we've made it to the important part! You already know that the purpose of your Scholarship Express Package is to help you apply for scholarships quickly and efficiently, but, HOW? Follow these steps to make the application process as fast and painless as possible:

1. As soon as you've got a fresh, new scholarship application in your hand (or on your computer screen), immediately flip your binder open to your Scholarship Deadline Sheet and get that sucker filled out.

2. Complete the actual application. Whether you access it online, scan it into your computer and create a PDF file with interactive form fields, answer the questions in black ink, or feed it into your grandmother's ancient typewriter, you need to fill out the information requested on the application pages. You won't have to go searching for the answers, because all of this data should be readily available right inside of your SEP binder!

You might say, "The application only gives me six short lines to list my interests, but I've created an awesome clubs/activities resume with twelve items on it. Should I attach this form to my application?" The answer to this question is "no." Remember that the scholarship committee will be evaluating hundreds—possibly thousands—of applications! If they only want six, one-word answers during the preliminary round, that's all you should give them. Pick your most *interesting* interests to showcase and/or the ones that fit best with the type of scholarship or the purpose of the sponsoring organization.

3. Gather any extra pages that you are asked to submit along with your application. For instance, the committee may request items such as a copy of your school transcript or your SAT scores. This is where you HOPE that you are invited to attach the cool resumes you've created for your activities, community service, and work experience!

4. Pick an essay. You may need to write a fresh one, but chances are that you already have an appropriate composition in your portfolio that is ready—or almost ready—to shove inside your envelope and mail away!

If you need to adapt or revise one of your essays, this is where your nifty USB flash drive comes into play. Plug it into your computer, do a little bit of word processing, and within minutes (in most cases) you'll be printing out an essay that fits perfectly with your current scholarship application needs. Here are some examples of revisions you may need to make to your essay of choice:

a. You may need to reformat your essay to match the guidelines provided in the application packet. The committee might ask that you include the name of their organization in the upper corner; they may request a certain type of spacing or font; they might want everybody's essay to share the same title, etc.

b. You may need to adjust the word count on your essay. Let's say you've composed a 700-word piece on your experiences as a day camp counselor for underprivileged kids. If a certain scholarship asks you to "Describe a time when you've shown leadership qualities" in 500 words or less, you have the option of simply editing the similar essay that you've already written. Alternately, if you have not been given a word limit this time, or if it is a higher number than before, you may want to jazz up an old essay and make it even longer and more exciting!

c. You might decide to adapt a previous essay so that it more closely relates to the provided topic or to the purpose of the organization. For example, you are applying for a scholarship that is being awarded only to future students of chemistry, and the essay question is "How can we use chemistry to make a positive impact on the world?" For a previous scholarship, you wrote an essay about your plan to enter the field of drug research, and titled it "My Goal for the Future: Better Treatments for Genetic Illness." With a few changes here and there, this same essay can form the base for a new version called "Cured by Chemistry: Future Innovations in Drug Research."

5. Time to whip out that USB drive again, so you can make adjustments to your letters of recommendation. Do this, of course, only to the extent agreed upon between you and the people who wrote your letters. The revisions you make may be as simple as changing the name of the organization in the heading, or personalizing the salutation. In the extreme case that you need a letter that is geared in a whole new direction, the portability of your flash drive will serve you well. Which of the following requests sounds more reasonable?

"Ms. Lebrowski, could you write me another scholarship recommendation letter, please? This time, talk about what a great job I did serving on the student council and how I was in charge of fundraising for the class trip."

Or

"Ms. Lebrowski, I want to thank you again for the wonderful recommendation letter that you wrote on my behalf. I have a copy of it right here on this portable drive, and I was wondering if you might have some time to add a paragraph that describes my leadership skills for submission to the Future Administrators of America scholarship competition?"

6. You should now have collected each document that you need for your application packet, with most (or even ALL) of it found right inside your SEP binder. The final step is to put everything into an addressed and stamped envelope and mail it away!

But, not until you've made your copies...

The Scholarship Follow-Up File

As previously mentioned, you should always save complete copies of every scholarship application that you submit. You will need these records for various follow-up activities.

The easiest way to keep track of your finished applications is to get yourself a portable file cabinet that will accommodate hanging folders. These containers are affordable, easy to obtain, available in a variety of exciting colors, and made of durable plastic. Yes, I realize that plastic is not an entirely indestructible substance, but unlike your old Barbie dolls or G.I. Joe action figures, your file cabinet will not fit in a microwave oven. If you are VERY serious about protecting your completed scholarship applications, feel free to invest in a fireproof safe.

Organizing your finished applications is as simple as labeling the top of each folder with the name of the scholarship and sticking all the matching paperwork inside. You can place these folders with the first scholarship you applied to at the front of the cabinet, or in alphabetical order for easy reference. Or you can file them in order of how many paper cuts you suffered while filling each one out. I don't care. The point is that you are keeping all the old applications safely in one place!

Your next step to complete after you've sent away each application is a simple check mark on your Scholarship Deadline Sheet to indicate that you've finished the job (as if you could forget after all that hard work…but, trust me, checking that box will give you as great a feeling of satisfaction as finally convincing your dad to stop for a bathroom break during a long road trip with a 7-11 Big Gulp). Remember to record the date of the mailing on your spreadsheet.

Wait for about a week…

Now it's time to check in with the scholarship organization to ask if they have received your application. The purpose of this contact is three-fold. Of course, you do honestly want to reassure yourself that your application arrived safely; it wasn't lost in the mail or delivered to the wrong department. The next benefit is that, after digging your application out of the middle of the pile, the committee member is almost guaranteed to glance through the pages as she checks to make sure that the packet really is yours. Afterward, she will place it back on the top of the stack, where the application may receive even further exposure. Voila! You have made your entry just a little more memorable!

Which communication medium should you use to inquire about the safe delivery of your scholarship application: telephone or e-mail? As quick and easy as it is to hit the "Contact Us" button on the organization's website, my preference is definitely for using the phone. Actually speaking to someone is more personal, more memorable, and provides more opportunity to establish a rapport with a person on the scholarship team. You've attached a voice and a personality to your name, which is just one small step away from a face-to-face conversation. A telephone exchange also lends itself to more elaborate communication than a short e-mail reply reading: "Yes, (insert your name here), we have received your application." If you are lucky, the person whom you are speaking with may take a moment to look over your application and ask a couple of questions. Yes!!! You just scored yourself a mini-interview! (To prepare for this possibility, read through the next chapter).

While the scholarship committee is (hopefully) learning a little bit about you, you also have the opportunity to find out more about them. You definitely want to write down and remember the name of the person you spoke with, for future friendliness, but also make sure to ask about any timelines that have been established for selecting the scholarship winner(s). Here is an example of a nice, polite follow-up telephone conversation with a scholarship committee member:

```
"Hello, this is Lisa with (organization
name)."

"Hi, Lisa, my name is Felecia Hatcher. I am one
of the high school students hoping to win your
(name) scholarship. I'm placing this follow-up
call to check and make sure that my application
has made it into the hands of the correct
people. Do you know who I should be speaking to
about the status of my application?"

"I can help you with that. Excuse me for one
moment while I check our file. You said your
name is Felecia Hatcher, correct?"

"Yes, thank you."

(Wait on hold. Listen to music)

"Hello again, Felecia. Yes, I have your
```

application right here in my hand, so it made it to the right place."

"Great! Thank you so much for checking."

"You're welcome. Oh, I see here that you've been a member of the 4-H club for several years! I was a 4-Her, too! I rode and trained horses as a kid back home in Texas. What do you do in your 4-H club?"

I raise show rabbits in our backyard. It's one of the few types of animal husbandry that I could pull off while growing up in the suburbs."

"You must really love your rabbits. I'm reading here on your application about how many prize ribbons they've won!"

"Yes, my rabbits are definitely my babies, but, really, what I like best about 4-H is all of the volunteer work that our club does in the community."

"I agree. In Texas, we used to gather up our gentlest horses and organize a fun rodeo every summer for the disabled kids at a nearby camp. It was the highlight of the year for everybody."

"I bet. That sounds great! (pause) Well, thanks so much for checking on my application, Lisa. Do mind if I ask one more question?"

"Of course not, go right ahead."

"When does your scholarship committee expect to make a decision about who they will award?"

"The other judges and I need to have the ten

best applicants selected by March 18th. We'll schedule first-round interviews beginning the following Monday."

"Thanks for the information; maybe I'll even be one of those lucky finalists! Thanks again, Lisa. It was very nice meeting you, and I hope we get a chance to talk again someday."

"I'd enjoy that, Felecia. Have a good day."

(P.S. I've never really raised bunny rabbits. This was a fictional example.)

When you've finished your follow-up call, record all the information that you learned in your SEP binder. You need to know which days to be waiting nervously beside the phone.

A week or two after the deadline for submitting scholarship applications has passed by, you should send the organization a Thank You-card in the mail. Express your appreciation that they are considering you for their generous scholarship, and thank them for the work they are doing to make the world a better place. Anything simple and polite will suffice to remind the committee who you are. Once this task is completed and recorded, all you can do is wait and wonder.

Why is it so important to follow-up on your scholarship applications? You might be thinking that it's better not to bother the organization and make a nuisance of yourself. Don't worry about that! As long as you are friendly and courteous, nobody will be upset about your interference. Making contact with the committee not only cements your name into someone's head, but the act is also a demonstration of your proactive spirit and determination to win their scholarship. They want to award their money to someone who really wants and needs it, so show them how important their competition is to YOU. If you are lucky, you will be a reason to open your file box and dig out that old, half-forgotten scholarship application—because you've been invited to interview as a finalist!

Bonus Hint: You should follow-up with job applications just as diligently as you do with your scholarships. In both cases, most people don't take the time to do this, so your keen interest and sense of responsibility will usually earn you an edge over the competition!

Put On a Happy Face(Book)— The Social Media Alert!

After (or even before) you mail out that first scholarship application, you should set aside an hour or so to investigate and (if necessary) clean-up your online presence. Take note of how many times throughout this book I advise you to research the scholarship organization to learn more about them? There's a good chance that the judges might do the same thing to you! What dirty not-so-secrets will they find out about you after fifteen minutes of browsing the Internet? If you are shuddering at the thought, follow these tips for "scrubbing" your Web reputation squeaky clean:

1. Google every possible variation of your name. If anything unbecoming pops up about you, see if it's something you can have taken down. You want the committee to find only re-posted news articles about your good deeds and awards, not the joke page your best friend set up back in middle school that describes your fictional exploits of you stealing from the corner store.

2. Check your social media sites (Facebook, MySpace, LinkedIn, Twitter, Flickr, Blogger, etc.). If all your content is dignified and academic, meaning serious, grammatically correct blog posts about social issues, quotes from famous people that you admire, poetry you've written (not the dirty limericks), etc., then you are just fine. Your social networking profiles will prove an asset to your cause. If your pages do not make you appear "smart," "mature," and "hardworking," do you have the time to fix at least one of them so that it will show you in your best light? Snooping scholarship judges will be more impressed at finding something flattering about you than if they uncover nothing at all.

3. For web pages that are impossible to "scrub," make sure they stay hidden from sight. Try to use nicknames to create your profiles, and always keep your privacy settings fixed so people must be "friended" or approved somehow before they can get inside. Even so, log out and check what information appears on your default profile page (the place where it says, "You must be this person's friend to view any more information," or something to that effect). Your picture will probably show up there, so you might want to delete the shot taken at THAT party, and replace it with one of you sitting demurely on a park bench with a sweet smile and your head cocked adorably to the side. It may also help to have a puppy sitting on your lap.

4. Get those videos off of YouTube. Right now. You know which ones I mean.

5. Stay vigilant, because your web presence might be clean as a whistle on Tuesday, but a total mess after Saturday night. Watch what sort of photos/videos other people are posting and tagging with your name. Yes, it was totally awesome how you jumped over your grandpa on your skateboard after he fell asleep at the family BBQ, but, unless you've applied for a skateboarding scholarship, this isn't the type of accomplishment you want to showcase for the judges. Some search engines allow you to set up alerts to warn you each time your name pops up on the Web. Use them!

6. Most importantly check your voicemail. If your ringback tone is "Drop it Like it's Hot," you might as well drop your scholarship chances like its hot. Keep it professional so you don't scare off scholarship judges.

Now, keep your fingers crossed that no crazy party people have the same name as you!

Notes

Notes

_____

_____

_____

_____

_____

_____

_____

_____

_____

_____

_____

_____

_____

_____

_____

_____

_____

_____

_____

_____

_____

_____

_____

Chapter Seven
How to Become an Interview Rock Star!

YES!!!! You've received a letter or a phone call congratulating you for being a scholarship finalist! You feel like you're on the very top of the world and looking straight down into a gaping chasm of despair and distress. This particular scholarship committee is not willing to simply read over your application and write out a check—they actually want to MEET you in *person*!

I'm not ashamed to admit that I was a little bit shocked and very unprepared when I was called in for my first interview. The competition was for a huge chunk of college money—$10,000—from a successful insurance company that had a local subsidiary in the town where I lived. My interview was scheduled for December, not too far off from Christmas. Wasn't this supposed to be a happy time of year? So, why was I terrified?

When I got to my interview, I found out that I competing against another girl for the scholarship. It just so happened that I'd known my competitor since we were five years old. We'd attended school and Girl Scouts together almost our entire lives! I knew my friend would put up a good fight for this scholarship, because my comrade in cookie sales was one tough cookie herself. We had similar backgrounds as far as clubs and community service, but her grades were really good—better than mine, for sure.

It turned out that the questions for this interview were really kind of dry, basically just re-covering the things I'd written in my application. They asked me about my life experiences, my aspirations, and a few more questions about my personal history. I walked out of there feeling pretty good, like I knew I nailed it.

Unfortunately, I'd nailed nothing. My first chance at winning a major scholarship turned into my first major disappointment. I blame my failure on the fact that I hadn't yet learned how to *really* turn on the charm and sell my awesome self to the scholarship committee. These are the skills that I intend to teach you in this chapter, so that YOUR first scholarship interview can be an amazing success!

At this point, you are probably thinking back to Chapter Four, and saying, "Whaddya mean writing an essay is the scariest part of the scholarship application? This face-to-face stuff is WAY worse!"

Okay, you got me. It probably is worse. But, c'mon, the pain is worth it, right? Nothing in life is ever *totally* free!

Who knows, you might be one of the luckier scholarship winners out there. You may have been blessed with a bubbly personality and an enthusiasm for social get-togethers that just won't quit. Maybe spending an afternoon chatting with a bunch of strangers in a high-pressure environment is *exactly* what you pick to do if given a choice of activities. And even if you're not a social butterfly, maybe you'll be awarded a scholarship that doesn't require an interview to win. Not all of them do. If this is the case, you'll probably never bother to read this chapter at all!

We are going to continue on the assumption that after you sent out all those expertly completed application forms, your phone began ringing off the hook with offers for interviews. You're excited, but a little bit nervous at the same time and you are desperately in need of my sage advice.

The Five 'P's of Professionalism

Learning to behave in a professional manner is a skill that will benefit you in multiple facets of your life. Whether it be a job promotion, a membership to a prestigious country club, a nomination for a presidency, or even just clearance to adopt a puppy from your local animal shelter, getting what you want often means impressing the right people. While the specifics of professional behavior will vary in different situations, there are general rules that should always be followed when meeting with people who hold the keys to your dreams. I call them the "Five 'P's of Professionalism," and I will explain what each one means in relationship to acing your scholarship interviews:

I. Preparation

As the Boy Scout motto encourages, you should always "Be Prepared" before you sit down for a scholarship interview. The first thing you should do after receiving notification that you are a finalist, is to go running to your file box so you can look over the application that impressed the judges enough to single YOU out from the crowd. You need to remind yourself of what questions they asked you, and which information you supplied for them, for example, the essay you sent, letters of recommendation, etc.

Next, it's time to research the generous organization that is sponsoring this scholarship. You may have done a bit of spying already, when you were designing your application to match their values, but now it's time to dig even deeper! Learn all that you can about the organization and the staff who work there, beginning with a through reading of their website. If somebody called you to set up a meeting place and time, you may have had the foresight to ask how the interview would be conducted, and by whom. If you did not get this information, you can also call the organization to ask a few questions just try not to sound like you are investigating them with the tenacity of the CIA! You ARE spying on them, of course, but don't be too obvious about it. And once you figure out the names of the organization's key members, be sure to look up their Facebook pages! Anything you can find out about the people/causes behind the scholarship will help you to know which of your qualities or activities are in closest alignment with whatever they stand for.

Now would be a good time to straighten up your SEP binder, and make sure that all the documents are updated and neatly in order. You will want to take this valuable resource with you to the interview, so that you can:

a. Show off your organizational skills

b. Be ready with extra materials about yourself, should you be asked to provide any

Here's an example of how your SEP binder could come in handy:

On their application, the scholarship committee may have asked for the only most basic information about your extracurricular activities—or maybe they didn't ask about them at all. During the interview, one of their questions might be: "What is your favorite hobby and why?"

This inquiry would provide you with an excellent opportunity to whip out copies of your annotated "Activities Resume" and pass them around. You might say something like, "As you can see from this sheet, I enjoy different interests. But, I think my *favorite* pastime is…"

Whether it happens during the interview or afterward, the members of the committee are sure to glance over the page you've handed them, so they will see what an active and passionate person you are!

Another important way to prepare for your interview is to review commonly asked questions, and practice answering them in an interview-type setting. I will talk about this further on in the chapter.

2. Presentation

When you meet the scholarship committee, you want to look *gooood*! There's no need to go totally formal, like you did for the Senior Prom, but the judges are going to want to see a person who is neatly dressed and immaculately groomed. Yes, I'm encouraging you to take a bath.

Arriving at an interview (of any kind) looking your best is simply a matter of respect. Your appearance tells the organization what you think of their worthiness, and you don't want to show up wearing tattered sneakers, which will give the impression you don't take their scholarship seriously. It doesn't matter if the committee already knows that you are not a fancy individual, but you will still be expected to act and dress professionally. If you are applying for a surfing scholarship, that's still no excuse to show up soaking wet and wearing nothing but a pair of Bermuda shorts. If you are interviewing with a member of the American Quarter Horse Association, you should still take off your muddy cowboy boots and wash the hay out of your hair before making your appearance. If you are a contender for a literary scholarship, sure, go ahead and make the meeting memorable by dressing up like William Shakespeare. Just make sure that your breeches are neatly pressed and your ruff is properly starched!

3. Punctuality

A key component of professionalism is showing up for appointments on time. Scholarships are a business proposition, and nobody in the business world wants to wait and get behind in schedule!

Use these five tips to make sure you get to your interview on time:

1. **Gather everything you need the night before.** 7 a.m. on the morning of your 9 a.m. interview is NOT the time to discover that you don't have any pantyhose without runs, or that one of your dress shoes has mysteriously gone missing. Make sure in advance that your clothes are ready to put on and any additional materials you plan to take are waiting next to the front door.

2. **Allow PLENTY of time.** Plan to depart a good half an hour sooner than what is actually necessary to allow for unexpected delays. If you arrive at your destination far too early, that's great! You can use the extra time to rehearse answers in your head or to do breathing exercises to calm your nerves.

3. **Take traffic issues into account.** When you are deciding what time you will leave the house, carefully consider your destination and the route you must take to get there. The directions you looked up on Google maps might say that the journey will only take 20 minutes, but your computer does not know that you will be driving in the middle of morning rush hour. Google is also unaware that Fifth Street has been under reconstruction for the past month, after it was torn up by the landing of an alien spaceship that the army whisked away almost before you managed to snap a picture of it with your cell phone. Expect delays.

4. **Know where you are going.** It may not be enough to have printed off a set of directions from the Internet. Your computer will not be able to tell you things like how difficult it is to find parking near the building, or that the organization's office is all the way up on the eighth floor. These little details can turn what should have been a relaxed journey into a frantic rush to make it to your appointment in time. A wise idea would be to take a

practice drive to the site of your interview ahead of time. If you do this at the same time of day when you will need to travel later, not only will you know PRECISELY where the office is located, but you will get a preview of the actual traffic situation and any areas of possible highway construction.

5. **Show off your punctuality.** Enter the office exactly 10 minutes before the scheduled time of your interview. This will show everyone in the organization that you are a responsible person who allows him/herself plenty of time to arrive for appointments, but if you appear inside the office any earlier, you are just a pest! If your interviewer(s) happens to be available ahead of schedule, the person will no doubt appreciate the opportunity your promptness has granted for beginning and ending the proceedings early. Business people just love to be AHEAD of schedule!

What if you are late, despite the very best of intentions? Well, if something totally unpredictable happens, and you know you'll be arriving even five minutes late, use these tactics to mitigate the damage to your reputation:

1. **When in doubt, call.** Have the organization's phone number on hand, so you can call from the road if something holds you up during your drive. Even if you just think you might be late, go ahead and place a warning call. Leaving a message along the lines of, "I'm on my way, but traffic is heavier than usual, so there's a possibility that I might be ten to fifteen minutes late," is not a bad thing to do at all! Your interviewer will be impressed by your considerate nature whether or not you actually do arrive late. If you are running just a tiny bit behind schedule, you may think that it's better to push harder and just hope that you'll make it on time, but this is not a good idea. If you do wind up arriving late, you've missed the opportunity to be polite and proactive by alerting the committee in advance. If you are on time after all, you'll still get bonus points for courtesy and professionalism that you wouldn't have received otherwise.

2. **Show consideration for the interviewer's busy schedule.** Let the committee know that you are flexible and that you are concerned more about their valuable time than you are your own. If you are going to be significantly late, make it clear that you will adapt to whatever solution will work best for THEM, even if it means re-scheduling for a different day or waiting around their office until they have time to fit you in later.

3. **Consider your excuses before you make them.** It's always polite to provide an explanation for tardiness, but remember that your excuse can reflect poorly on you as a scholarship candidate. If you can't say anything good, don't say anything at all! Here are some examples of the type of excuses you should avoid:

   a. Excuses that make you seem irresponsible and unreliable, such as "I couldn't find my car keys."

   b. Excuses that give the committee TMI (Too Much Information), such as, "My dog vomited all over our living room and Mom wouldn't let me leave until I cleaned everything up."

   c. Excuses that aren't true, such as "I'm late because my grand-mother died just as I was putting on my tie."

   d. Excuses that SOUND like lies, such as, "I saw a little kid get hit by a truck, so I stopped to perform CPR until the paramedics arrived."

Unless you have proof to back up your story, like a shirt covered in blood, or a TV news interview that will air later, don't try to pull off an outrageous excuse for tardiness—even if it's totally true!

4. **Apologize, but don't grovel.** Whether you have a valid excuse to offer, or simply say, "I'm so sorry that I'm late," apologize sincerely, but don't dwell on the mistake by brow-beating yourself. Make it easy for the scholarship committee to move on and start discovering the GOOD things about you!

4. Personality

I'm sure you've already heard all the standard advice about making a good first impression:

○ Firm handshake

○ Eye contact

○ Pleasant demeanor etc.

In addition to acting friendly and personable overall, you should look for opportunities to dedicate a little time and attention to your interviewer(s). Yes, the purpose of the interview is to help the committee know you better, but there's no need to be completely self-centered. Your interviewer is a PERSON, just like you, and you want to make a connection with this person that leaves positive memories in his/her mind. The interview will probably start out relaxed, and the opening chit-chat period is a great time to show interest in the person representing the organization. You might ask your interviewer how long she's been working with the company and what she enjoys most about the job. Or maybe he will have a picture of his pet collie on his desk, and you can mention how your aunt had one when you were growing up, and it was the smartest dog that you've met to date. Little things like this can spark conversations that will make you and your interviewer feel comfortable with each other.

If your interviewer volunteers personal information about herself, show interest rather than simply brushing the comment aside and continuing to brag about yourself. Here's an example:

Interviewer: "I see here on your application that you've won several windsurfing competitions. I tried that once on vacation, but I wasn't any good at it."

You: "It's a hard sport to learn unless the wind is just right. Where was it that you tried windsurfing?"

Other interviewing strategies are about the same as the skills a little girl must practice to compete in a pre-teen princess beauty pageant: smile a lot, appear confident on the outside even if your stomach is clenched with fear, and, if there is more than one person interviewing you, give equal attention to each of the judges.

5. Positivity

You are an enthusiastic person with dreams and goals that you feel passionate about. The scholarship committee wants to give its award to a person who they deem will be a success in life, but who is also happy and optimistic. Despite the fact that many people use cruel and cutthroat tactics to claw their way up the ladder of success, you don't want to act or sound like one of *them*. Over the course of your interview, avoid badmouthing anything or anyone. As you grin your way through the committee's interrogation, maintain the impression that your successful future will be surrounded by rainbows, unicorns, and sparkling rays of starlight. Optimism = Confidence = Professionalism.

As an extra expression of your enthusiasm and professionalism, make it a point to send the organization a brief Thank You-card or note after the completion of your interview. This revival of a dying courtesy will give the committee yet another opportunity to remember you and your winning smile. In your note, express your gratitude at being selected as a finalist, and talk about what a pleasure it was to meet everybody and to learn more about their organization.

Are You Glossophobic?

The odds are not in your favor. Statistics indicate that as many as three out of four people suffer from glossophobia, or speech anxiety. In survey reports, a staggering number of glossophobes say they fear public speaking more than they fear death.

Now, undergoing a scholarship interview is hardly equivalent to addressing an audience, but many of the same phobias and remedies apply. Even if you are not behind a podium, and even if you are being interviewed by only one person, the attention is still planted squarely on YOU, and this knowledge might make you very nervous.

Just Relax

If you are panicking about your scholarship interview, the first thing you should do is just take a deep breath and relax. I know this is easier said than done, but it helps to keep this one important fact in mind: the scholarship committee already likes you! They have singled you out for a reason—because your application impressed them. Knowing that you are already a favorite of the scholarship judges should give you the confidence you need to take a deep breath and march right into that interview with a smile on your face and your head held high and proud, but, if this endorsement is not quite enough, here are a few more confidence boosters:

○ Fear is a good thing. It keeps you alert and focused.

○ Even when people feel as if they are literally trembling from nervousness, their condition hardly shows outwardly.

○ Realize that you are not alone. Even famous celebrities, who are constantly in the public eye, are prone to suffering from stage fright. You don't believe me? Um, see the bullet point right above this one.

○ Hang in there, because even if you start out feeling distressed, you are almost guaranteed to relax as the interview progresses.

○ If you make obvious mistakes, you'll know what areas you'll get a chance to improve upon during the next interview.

○ Remain positive. Imagine the interview going really well. Tell yourself that you'll do great, and don't let bad public speaking experiences from the past consume you and zap your confidence. Tell yourself, "That happened before, but I can handle it NOW."

○ Get yourself excited about the opportunity you've been granted! You are an incredible person, and now you'll be having a conversation with people who want you to share your awesomeness with them. How flattering is that?

○ Exercise just before the interview (but allow yourself time to wash away the sweat). Exercise can get your endorphins going and your adrenaline coursing or it could exhaust so much that you don't have any energy left to be nervous and agitated. Try to avoid the latter, as it never helps your case to nod off to sleep during a scholarship interview.

○ Keep oxygenated. Breathe deeply and often, but not so often that you cross the line into hyperventilation. Passing out = not so good.

○ If you are religious, pray for peace and serenity; if you possess Zen-like powers, arrive early and mediate in your car before entering the interview.

○ If you feel super nervous, don't be afraid to admit it to your interviewer(s). You won't lose points if you say something like, "Please forgive me if I seem jittery. I know how important this interview is, so I'm a little bit nervous."

○ Unless you are being interviewed by a Hollywood movie star, DON'T picture the person in their underwear. Whatever you visualize will probably not be pretty.

Have I made you even more apprehensive? Now, maybe you are worried about *brand new* possibilities, like hyperventilating in front of the committee, or God ignoring your pleas for strength because of all those times you only pretended to drop your dollar into the church collection plate when you were a little kid. Calm down (seriously, don't hyperventilate YET), because I haven't yet shared with you the most amazing and foolproof way to beat your stage fright. It can be summed up in just one word: **PRACTICE**

How to Practice for Your Scholarship Interview

Like I've mentioned before, "practice makes perfect," and since we all know that "nobody's perfect," a little practice before entering a room filled with (very nice) scholarship piranhas is probably a great idea. Feeling like you're ready for anything that might be thrown at you is a component of "Preparation," the first of the five "professionalism Ps."

So, you wanna' know how to practice for a scholarship interview? Try following this series of steps:

1. Make out a list of commonly asked scholarships questions (I'll provide some examples later). Write down your answer to each question on a note card, and then read them over and over again to familiarize yourself with the things you'd like interviewer(s) to hear you say. Keep in mind that familiarize is not the same thing as memorize. You don't want to be SO prepared for the interview that you sound like a robot that's been programmed to say scholarly things about itself!

2. Find somebody to play the role of interviewer, and practice your answers out loud and with natural expressions and gestures. Show your partner the list of common questions, and ask him/her to choose five at random for the practice interview. Request that your volunteer also think up two more surprise questions for you that are NOT on the list, so you can practice coming up with intelligent answers out of thin air. If the person complains about not knowing what else to ask, tell him/her to start the question with "What is your favorite …?" or "What is your opinion on… (insert social issue here)?"

3. As you are play-interviewing, remember to practice both personality and positivity. Act as natural as is possible under the circumstance and hope that your volunteer doesn't start laughing so hard that it sets off your own fit of giggles.

4. After the interview, ask your partner if you did well, or not-so-great.

5. Play the video of your interview (you set up a recording device, right?), and try not to cringe as you watch yourself smile and brag. Ignore how you look, and concentrate on seeing yourself as a scholarship interviewer would see you. Can you spot any areas where you need to improve your performance?

6. Repeat the first five steps as many times as it takes to help you feel comfortable with the interview process. If possible, try and arrange to "interview" with someone you don't know very well (or not at all!) to best simulate the awkwardness you'd experience in a *real* interview situation.

The Dreaded Interview Questions

You'll find that the questions the scholarship committee asks during their interview are very similar to those they set as essay topics. Here is a list of variations upon the most common interview questions…

Questions about yourself and your life experiences:

○ What is your greatest strength and weakness?

○ Who has most influenced your life and why?

○ What do you consider your biggest success in life thus far?

○ What is your favorite thing about the family you grew up in?

○ What two adjectives best describe you?

○ Tell me (us) about a personal achievement that makes you proud.

○ Tell me (us) about a mistake that you made and what you learned from it.

Questions about your interests and activities:

○ What is the best experience you've had while performing community service?

○ Why do you enjoy competing in _____?

○ Why did you select _____ as your sport of choice?

○ What is your favorite book?

○ What kind of music do you enjoy the most?

○ How did you spend your last summer vacation?

Questions about your education and future:

○ What are your career goals?

○ Why do you want to enter the field of _____?

○ Tell us about an accomplished person in your field of study who you admire.

○ I see you plan to attend _____. Why did you choose this college?

○ How will you use your education for the betterment of the world?

○ Where do you see yourself in five years? Ten years?

Questions about random topics seeming unrelated to you or the scholarship:

○ What famous person—living or dead—would you most like to meet?

○ Which past president do you believe did the most for our country?

○ Do you know the name of your state governor? Members of Congress? Mayor?

○ What would you most like to change about the world?

○ If you had to leave the United States, what country would you like to live in?

Obviously, any "random" questions that your interviewer throws at you will be somewhat unpredictable. The topics might be about current events, social concerns, or other things that an alert and intelligent teenager should be aware of and have contemplated at great length (yeah, right). Think of these questions as the type that might be asked to a contestant in a Miss America competition. Hey, if she can answer them without letting her mile-wide smile waver, so can you!

What's in the news right now? Are there any interesting controversies that you might be expected to have an opinion about? Think global, national, and local. Also, refresh yourself on the latest developments with our ongoing social/political issues, such as abortion, gay marriage, and immigration law.

What Makes a Good Answer?

If you want to deliver impressive answers, think of each interview question as its own mini-essay. Before you write out your planned replies to the list of common questions, go back and review the Chapter Four guidelines on how to compose a winning essay. The same rules apply to interview questions. I'll provide a very brief review:

○ Be honest and true to yourself

○ Strive for creative and unique answers

○ Be positive and passionate

○ Don't volunteer information that reflects badly upon yourself as a person

When you eat at a Chinese restaurant, do you and your friends play the game where you tack on the words "in bed" to the end of your cookies' fortunes? There is a similar habit you should develop when processing the questions asked at a scholarship interview. The most important rule of thumb is to remember that whether or not the person asks it specifically, you should always add the words "and why?" to the end of every question.

For example:

- ❍ "What kind of music do you enjoy the most?" ("And Why?")

- ❍ "What are your career goals?" ("And Why?")

- ❍ "How did you spend your summer vacation?" ("And Why?")

Oh, wait…that last one doesn't work.

The point I am trying to make is that no matter how quickly and simply you CAN answer a question, just DON'T. The committee wants more than a one-word or even one-sentence response out of you! They expect you to deliver a mini-essay, remember? Obviously, you don't need to think up an introduction, body, and conclusion all on the fly. That's where the "mini" part kicks in. The main goal of your abridged essay answer is to BACK UP the point you are making with pertinent facts. To this end, the word "Because" is the best buddy and constant companion of the phrase "And Why?"

The significance of "Why" and "Because" is that by combining the two you can reveal qualities about yourself that the scholarship committee wants to see. Before they decide to pay for your education, they need to feel confident that you will be a success in life and that their money won't be wasted. No matter the question asked, your interviewer will be looking for the underlying personal qualities that are expressed by your choice of answer. Don't make these qualities hard to uncover. Assure the sponsors of your worthiness by allowing each of your answers to explain why you are a capable person who will go out into the world and thrive, not just survive. Try to determine which of your positive qualities this particular scholarship committee will value the most, and then make sure that your reply to each question gives them something they really want to hear. Your answers should scream out least one of these things:

- ○ I am an enthusiastic and passionate person.
- ○ I am goal-oriented.
- ○ I am a good person who cares about the world.
- ○ I know what I want out of life.
- ○ I don't allow obstacles to stand in the way of my dreams.
- ○ I face challenges head on.
- ○ I understand what it will take to succeed in the career of my choice.
- ○ I get along well with others.
- ○ I am determined and dedicated.
- ○ I want to right the wrongs in this world.
- ○ I have confidence in myself and my abilities.

In case you aren't usually the talkative type, here are a few examples of how to use the word "because" to turn your interview answers into useful information for the committee:

"What is your favorite book?"

BAD ANSWER = "It's Little Women."

GOOD ANSWER = "My favorite book is Little Women, BECAUSE I admire the strength of the four sisters as they battle the adversities in their lives, both big and small. Although the March girls grew up a long time ago, I find that I can relate to the way they feel about things, even though they talk differently and they almost live in a different world from mine. I think that says a lot about how human beings share a common experience throughout time and place. If I understand girls who lived in back in the 1800's, I know that I can also bond with people who live in other countries, or who are a different age or gender than me. Knowing this makes me more open to seeking friendships outside of my comfort zone, and I believe that my ability to see beyond a person's outward appearance will help me form meaningful relationships with everyone I meet in life."

"What is your favorite subject in school?"

BAD ANSWER = "I like art."

GOOD ANSWER = "I'm not especially artistic, but I really enjoy my art classes BECAUSE I like hands-on activities where I can feel a physical connection to my work. That's why I know I will be a great environmental scientist. I look forward to a career that will put me out in the field collecting samples or in a laboratory performing hands-on tests and experiments."

"What is the best thing about your family?"

BAD ANSWER = "We went on a lot of vacations."

GOOD ANSWER = "Our family vacations were always lots of fun, BECAUSE nothing ever seemed to go as planned. We could almost count on catastrophe, but we could also count on each other to band together and ride out the storm. I learned from my family that problems are best conquered by working as a team. For example, there was one time when…"

You might think it's too daunting a task to come up with shrewd answers to ALL of the common interview questions listed in this book, but it's really not as bad as it seems. Like with essays, many of them can be adapted to serve multiple purposes. For instance, if you decide that the two adjectives that describe you best are "persistent" and "resourceful." then you already have an answer to questions like:

- ○ "What are your greatest strengths?"

- ○ "What qualities will help you to be a great preschool teacher?"

- ○ "How will you deal with the difficulties of being a full time student?"

Although, preparing complete answers to common questions (but not memorizing them!) is very beneficial, even just thinking about what you could be asked, and maybe jotting down a few notes, can be enough to give you an edge over the competition.

How to Deal with Difficult Questions

What do you do if you are asked a question that baffles you despite all of your hard preparation? In the next chapter, you'll read about a time when I got stuck answering a series of tough questions that totally threw me off my game. I didn't handle the interview well (and I didn't get the scholarship that time), but I hope you can learn from my mistakes and do better in a similar situation.

I was dead meat from the very beginning that time, because I didn't have good answers to any of their questions, but it's unusual to be hit with such a difficult interview. More likely, you will be doing just fine until a particularly tough topic tackles you from out of nowhere. If you don't understand the question, don't be afraid to ask for clarification. You won't seem "dumb" because you seek full understanding before committing to an answer. That's what SMART people do!

If you simply don't know how to answer a question, just admit it. Being upfront about your shortcomings is better than trying to fake intelligence or insight. Respond with something like, "I've honestly never thought about this before, but off the top of my head, I would have to say …" Another option is to tell your interviewer, "I need a little bit of time to think about my answer to your question. Would it be possible for us to move on for now, and return to this subject later?" The committee will probably be happy to oblige, but don't go this route if you think that you will be distracted throughout the remainder of the interview as you desperately try to form a good answer in the back of your mind.

Maybe I can deflect some potential panic by preparing you for some of the more difficult questions scholarship interviewers might throw at you:

"Tell us about yourself."

This request can come as a shock if you walked into the interview mentally rehearsing the answers to specific questions. Maybe the committee really wants to hear you describe yourself in your own words, but more likely the tactic is an exercise in laziness (but don't bring up this possibility). If you come prepared, having control of the interview can work to your advantage. It's like writing your own recommendation letter! Before you arrive at any scholarship interview, first make a list of the accomplishments that you would most like the committee to know more about. What subjects can you discuss with the most passion and energy? Which of your many great qualities is the most spectacular? Being granted an opportunity to throw out your best material right in the beginning will save you the trouble of formulating your answers to steer the conversation toward your attributes most deserving of the interviewer's attention.

Why are you the best choice to receive our scholarship?

This is the slightly antagonistic version of the more pleasant, "Tell us about yourself." The question sounds like you've been issued a challenge to prove yourself in an arena of combat, but it essentially boils down to the same thing: You get a chance to present your very best qualities and accomplishments to the committee! Resist the impulse to say "Because I have no other way to get money," and run down your mental list of "essential interview topics." Anything and everything good about you works as a reason why you deserve to be awarded the scholarship.

Is there anything else you would like to add?

They asked, so it's not bragging if you bring up some great accomplishment that was overlooked during the course of the interview. AGAIN, mentally review the personal agenda you created for this meeting. What's left on it that you haven't had a chance to present yet? Tell them about it now.

To demonstrate how similar those last three questions really are, I'll give you an example of how easy it is to adapt the same idea to fit with as an answer for each one:

Q: "Tell us about yourself."

A: "I am a very resourceful and persistent person. One thing I've noticed about myself is that I can always find a creative way to get a job done, and I never stop trying until my problem is solved or my goal is reached." Etc.

This becomes …

Q: "Why are you the best choice to receive our scholarship?"

A: "If I win, I know that I will put your scholarship to good use and succeed with my education, because I am a very resourceful and persistent person. One thing I've noticed about myself is that I can always find a creative way to get a job done, and I never stop trying until my problem is solved or my goal is reached. These are qualities that will assist me greatly in a college environment." Etc.

This becomes …

Q: "Is there anything else you would like to add?"

A: "We've talked about so much already, but I did also want to mention to you that I am a very resourceful and persistent person. If I win, I know that I will put your scholarship to good use and succeed with my education, because I can always find a creative way to get a job done, and I never stop trying until my problem is solved or my goal is reached. These are qualities that will assist me greatly in a college environment." Etc.

Do you have any questions for us?

Yes, you do! Make sure that you are prepared with something, just in case this query is made (and you can ask your questions, even if it's not).

However, don't speak the thought that is most pressing the most on your mind: "When will I know if I've won your scholarship?" This is an unprofessional question! If they want you to know the timeframe of their final decision, they will volunteer this information before you leave.

As your interview is winding down, and you are invited to ask your questions, you should open with one about the group's organization and/or purpose. Start with something along the lines of "I was looking over your website before this interview, and I was wondering if you could tell me more about _____?" The committee has been very interested in learning about you, so it's only fair that you show an interest in them, too.

Another good question to ask might be: "Is there any more information or materials that I can provide to help you make your decision?" The answer will probably be, "No, we've got everything we need already," but you'll get extra points for your proactive attitude and generosity.

If you've got the guts for it, you could ask your interviewer, "Just so I know in the future, what did I do well in this interview, and what areas do I need to work on?" If the person is able to give you a thoughtful answer, this information will be highly beneficial to you. On the other hand, your interviewer might feel "put on the spot" by your inquiry, and you don't want to make this very important person feel uncomfortable! It's a judgment call.

Just one more thing before I wrap up this section… how should you respond to direct challenges or invitations to debate?

Probably, this won't happen, but there is a chance that you might get a question like, "If you are such a resourceful person, why do you need OUR scholarship in order to attend college?" or "Do you honestly believe that is the best solution to [insert popular social issue here]?" If someone chooses to challenge one of your answers, it is most likely because your interviewer wants to "test" your reaction to being placed under siege. Obviously, you need to remain cool, calm, and polite. Avoid acting flustered, angry, or defensive. Don't lose your smile, and answer the question as best you can in your most good-natured manner. If you are feeling "attacked," remind yourself that all of your competitors are being put through this same wringer, and think of it as a game that everyone is playing together. If you believe that you are being singled out for special attention because one of your statements might have struck a nerve with that particular person, you should still follow the advice given above. Instead of deciding that your interviewer hates you and giving up, use the disagreement as a chance to show the committee that you are an adaptable and open-minded person. Welcome the opinion of your challenger and listen to it respectfully. Maybe you will learn something new and have an opportunity to say, "You know, I think you may be right." If you remain unconvinced, be honest about that, too. You might say something like, "I still disagree, but you've made some valid points. You've given me a lot to think about." Don't despair, and assume that you've botched the interview by having your own opinion. If you handled yourself with dignity and grace, this little controversy might be the very thing that sets you apart from the others and makes your interview the most memorable!

Less Traditional Interviews

Group Interviews

It's possible that all of the finalists for a scholarship will be gathered together at one time to be interviewed as a group. You might be asked one question that you each answer in turn, or random questions might be thrown out to different participants. Either way, listen intently to the answers of your peers. Not only will your attentiveness be polite and professional, but you can also judge your competition and learn from their mistakes and triumphs.

Here are five tips for dealing with the challenges of a group interview.

1. Don't dominate the committee's time and attention.

2. Don't allow yourself to slip through the cracks.

3. Don't feel intimidated because you think your competition is superior to you.

4. Don't get overly cocky because you think your competition is inferior to you.

5. Do remember the names of your competitors so you can easily refer to them and their responses… "Like Michelle just said, I think that working with children is one of the most rewarding experiences that a person can have." "I agree with Aaron's opinion, but I also think it's worth mentioning that …"

Telephone Interviews

Sometimes it just isn't possible to interview for a scholarship in person, due to distance or the time constraints of the sponsoring committee. If you are offered a scholarship interview that is to be held over the phone, you will probably receive a preliminary call informing you that you are a finalist. If the person on the other end suggests the possibility of conducting the interview on the spot, politely respond that NOW IS NOT A GOOD TIME, and set up an appointment for a later date.

Why not just get the torture out of the way? Because you need to prepare, stupid! You need to go over your original application, research the organization, etc. When the time comes for your interview—even if it is the very next day—you can be ready.

Phone interviews may seem less "scary" than the face-to-face variety, because you are distanced from your interrogator. However, there are disadvantages to this distance, as it may be more difficult to bond and form a connection with person on the other end of the line. The key thing to remember is that you still need to practice PROFESSIONALISM to the same degree that you would in a more personalized situation. Follow these steps for phenomenal phone interviews:

1. Don't be late. You know exactly when your interviewer is scheduled to call, so BE THERE waiting next to the phone or computer.

2. Make sure that you are in a quiet location where you have complete privacy and you won't be interrupted. Barking dogs and crying little sisters kill professionalism as quickly as wearing a clown costume to a business meeting with an important client.

3. Sit up straight in a chair, as if you were in a face-to-face interview. Whether you believe it or not, lounging on a bed does change your whole tone and demeanor.

4. Dress up if you feel that looking professional will help you to act professional. Most definitely dress up if your interview will be a webcam or video conference. In this case, you must also be vigilant about the background that your interviewer(s) will be seeing. You don't want to appear sitting amidst the typical teenage mountain of dirty clothes and empty pizza boxes!

5. Take your enthusiasm up a notch. Smile like crazy, even if you can't be seen, because your happiness will come through in your voice. If your interviewer is unable to see your gestures and facial expressions, make your words and tone as expressive as you possibly can.

6. Finally, take advantage of your ability to use the answers you've written down as notes during the interview. They will come in very handy if your mind suddenly goes blank! However, you must take care not to sound like you are reading off a page. While preparing for your phone interview, you should spend some time practicing the art of using your notes while still speaking in a natural, spontaneous-sounding manner.

7. Send a thank-you note to the organization, just like you would after a face-to-face interview.

Notes

_____

_____

_____

_____

_____

_____

_____

_____

_____

_____

_____

_____

_____

_____

_____

_____

_____

_____

_____

_____

_____

_____

Notes

Chapter Eight
What Now?

You've won some scholarships or maybe you haven't. Either way, it's time to continue on with your life. You're going to have to figure out most of this without the help of a book, but I can give you a few valuable pointers to get you started. First, I'll talk to those of you who are heading off to college with a (figurative) pocket full of scholarships, and then I'll help out those of you who need to pay for your education some other way. Even scholarship winners can benefits from these extra ideas, because your winnings won't always cover all of your financial needs.

Get More Scholarships!

It's possible that you didn't win enough scholarships to cover your entire college tuition, but never fear! Just because you're out of high school, it doesn't mean you must quit applying to win scholarships. I had to get a few more during my college years, because my big scholarship did not cover study abroad or summer term.

You could even get lucky and win more money than you actually need for your tuition. In this case, the school will write you out a check! I used some of my extra scholarship money to put a down payment on a car. It really helps you to focus on your classes if you don't have to worry so much about earning money for life expenses.

The bad news about post-high school scholarships is that there are not as many opportunities out there as you had during your senior year. But the good news is that your chances of winning the ones that you DO find might be even better! It seems as though many people get lazy after they've started college and just fill out a quick loan application to cover the funding that they need. Others may not realize that they still qualify to win scholarship dollars. Whatever the reasons might have been, in my experience there was less competition for scholarships once high school was years behind me and the other applicants.

Keep Your Scholarships!

The first step in retaining your hard-earned scholarships is to do what you already planned to do all along—succeed and thrive in your new college environment.

Right, I know you weren't the greatest student in high school, but that doesn't mean you need to slip even further into mediocrity during your higher education. In many ways, college is even easier than high school. You will probably be taking fewer classes each quarter or semester, and they probably won't meet five times each week like high school civics and geometry used to. There is also more choice and flexibility. If you think best in the mornings when you are fresh, enroll in classes that begin at 8 a.m. However, if you're like me, stick with ones scheduled for noon or later!

The downside to having more freedom is that nobody is going to keep tabs on your academic status except YOU. You will need to take responsibility for your own success, because your instructors are not going to send home mid-term progress reports. Your mom won't be around to say "You're not going to the mall, young lady, until you've finished your homework," or to make a last-minute dash to the store to buy the poster board you need for your presentation the next day. Your dad's not going to quiz you on your periodic table of elements every morning during breakfast, or ground you indefinitely until you bring up that D in history.

It will be up to you to monitor yourself and find that perfect balance between study and partying with your friends. The key to this will be ORGANIZATION, which you were lucky enough to learn a lot about during the process of applying for multiple scholarships. Prepare yourself before you start college by practicing time management skills and developing effective ways to keep track of all your new responsibilities. Self-discipline is your new best friend!

On this note, you must take responsibility for knowing the eligibility requirements of any major scholarships you may have won. For instance, in order to keep my Community in Schools Scholarship, I had to maintain a (not-so-challenging) 2.0 GPA while in college. Here are some reasons why you might lose your hard-earned scholarships if you are not paying attention:

❍ Your GPA falls too low.

❍ You fail to enroll in a full-time load of classes.

❍ You drop out of the course of study that your scholarship supports.

❍ You leave the college that the scholarship allows you to attend.

❍ You quit the sport that earned you the scholarship.

❍ You use the scholarship money for expenses that are not authorized.

❍ You forget to apply for a continuation if the scholarship is renewable.

So, You Didn't Get a Scholarship... Go To College Anyway!

Just because you didn't win the first few scholarships that you applied for doesn't mean you should automatically hurl yourself into the ocean of blue-collar employment. You're still perfectly eligible to compete for award money, and some of the activities that you are doing to pay for your college education in the meantime may even give you a new edge over the competition.

I remember one particularly nerve-wracking scholarship competition that later helped me to believe in the old saying, "If at first you don't succeed, try, try again."

Because my mother belonged to this specific teachers' union, I qualified to apply for a scholarship offered by the Classroom Teachers Association. I was so excited when I got called in for an interview after submitting my application, because I figured this was easy money. I'd hit them with a smile, then I'd answer the typical questions about college, life goals, and my community service work—considering my life-long experience in manipulating a very smart teacher (my mom), I convinced myself that I could win this scholarship without so much as breaking a sweat!

As soon as I walked into the waiting room, I was handed a piece of paper and instructed to pick two questions from it that I wanted to answer. My interviewer would also pick two questions. At first glance, I thought maybe the sheet had been written in a foreign language! The list of questions included things like "What are your views on the inclusion policy?" and "Would you describe your political beliefs as conservative or liberal, and why?" The difficulty of the topics had me all dazed and confused! What the heck was I going to do? I decided to make a mad dash to my only refuge, good ol' Mom.

Although I was probably breaking about a bazillion rules, I excused myself to the bathroom and called Mom on my cell phone. As I stood whispering the list of questions to my mother, I felt almost certain that she would be able to help me ace this interview and sound super intelligent, but even a seasoned educator with a Ph.D. could not answer such tough questions off the top of her head. I left the bathroom stumped. Was that really my only chance at a *Who Wants to be a Millionaire?* lifeline?

I returned to the room, sweating bullets as I waited for them to call my name. My knees were knocking as I sat down in front of the two judges, but I suck it up and went through my usual elevator pitch with a big smile on my face. I spoke enthusiastically about my community service, my life, and my goals, but none of that mattered when it came time to answer their difficult questions. I did the best I could, but my stammered, uninformed answers were far from good enough win that scholarship.

The next year, as a freshmen at Lynn University, I gave the Classroom Teachers Association scholarship a second try. This time, I studied up on the topics in advance (yup, they asked the very same questions), and I aced the interview like a superstar! I walked away with 500 bucks to buy my textbooks for the next semester.

Remember that not all scholarships are limited to only current high school students. Never stop looking for the next opportunity to win college money, and never give up on your future!

More "Free" Money for College— Other Ways to Pay Your Way

Scholarships may be my favorite route to a free trip to college, but they are not the ONLY way! Our nation places a high value on the education of its citizens, and although tuition is expensive, plenty of opportunities are offered for those who are dedicated to obtaining a degree. Here are a few ideas you may want to consider:

Financial Aid

Many people think that they will only qualify to receive financial aid if their family receives food stamps and buys all of their clothes at Goodwill. This is a complete misconception, because even upper-middle class students may receive some financial aid. If you happen to come from a poor family, or have other complicating circumstances in your life, you may be able to finance your entire education solely on financial aid. A 19-year-old friend of mine, who was a former foster child and struggling single parent, had his entire tuition paid for by government grants, plus he also received a $2,000 check every quarter toward his school and living expenses. This may sound like a sweet deal, but please don't try to increase your financial aid allotment by having a kid! Babies cry while you're trying to study, and they drool on your term papers. It just isn't worth it.

What's the catch, you ask? Why would a college just give me free money? Well, in order to receive financial aid, you must complete the extensive Free Application for Federal Student Aid (FAFSA) or the CSS/Profile (private colleges). This initial step scares off the lazy students who don't like to fill out long forms, but that leaves more money in the pot for you, an organized individual, who is the veteran of so many scholarship applications.

What does "Pell Grant" mean? How about "Stafford Loan?" Are you worried about your ability to understand the complicated world of financial aid? Don't be, because you don't have to understand jack! Just turn your completed forms in at the school(s) of your choice, and let the experts handle the details. Of course, if you don't want to be completely clueless, there are plenty of websites and books that will teach you all about financial aid. This is one of them. If you don't believe me, close the cover for a second and check the title.

Well, okay…even if it isn't part of my job description, I'll give you a few tips on collecting all of the financial aid that you've got coming:

1. Be sure to get your income taxes done as soon as possible (or nag your parents about doing theirs), because you will need to supply that information on your financial aid application.

2. Hopefully, you've been accepted by more than one college. Before making a final decision, compare the amount/type of financial aid you can expect to receive from each institution. A more expensive school can easily become equally affordable (or even less costly) than one with a lower price tag, thanks to an awesome financial aid package.

3. Find out your schools' deadlines and turn in your application on time.

4. Ask your assigned financial aid officer to re-evaluate your package if you have a valid reason to think you haven't been offered enough help, or if your finances situation suffers a tragic blow.

5. Type "Summer Melt" into an Internet search engine and follow the instructions you find.

6. Get more help. Don't rely on only my advice to score the most you can possibly get in financial aid money. Visit www.fasfa.ed.gov for more information, and research the ways to best arrange your family finances before you apply.

Military Service

Just because *I* get sick to my stomach at the thought of waking up at 5 a.m. to run an obstacle course, doesn't mean that the military isn't a good option for YOU. There are many benefits that can be gained from enlisting in a branch of the U.S. Armed Forces, like job training, free travel, and the power trip you'll get from brandishing a huge gun. One of the best benefits for an education-minded person like you is Tuition Assistance (TA). In gratitude for your loyal service to your country, the military will foot (most of) the bill for your education during or after your tour of duty. In addition, being a military veteran will make you eligible to apply for even *more* scholarships than before, along with other educational programs such as college loan repayment. Best of all, they'll teach you discipline! Discipline is a very good thing to learn before heading off to college. The downsides of the military are bad food and a greater possibility of being shot than you would have staying home (depending on your home town, of course). Find out more at www.goarmyed.com.

AmeriCorps Volunteer Work

AmeriCorps offers you an opportunity to join one of their many community service programs throughout the United States. As a full or part-time member of the AmeriCorps network, you will earn a set amount of money to be used for college tuition or loan repayment. Here is an excerpt from their website:

"After successfully completing a term of service, AmeriCorps members who are enrolled in the National Service Trust are eligible to receive a Segal AmeriCorps Education Award. You can use your education award to pay education costs at qualified institutions of higher education, for educational training, or to repay qualified student loans."

Did you hop online and look up the amount of the Education Award? If so, you are probably thinking, "Why would I want to put in a full year's work to receive that relatively small amount of college money? I could earn more than that by working for 12 months at minimum wage!" While it's true that the award amount is not colossal, there are other benefits to joining AmeriCorps:

○ You will gain valuable life experience while helping others in need.

○ Your "valuable life experience" will look impressive on future scholarship applications and will give you material for insightful essays.

○ Being an AmeriCorps Alumni will make you eligible for additional scholarships.

○ Being an AmeriCorps Alumni will make you eligible for loan forgiveness.

○ Many colleges across the U.S. will match the amount of your AmeriCorps award.

○ Your assignment could help you progress further in your chosen career area.

○ Your living expenses are often covered while enrolled in AmeriCorps. How much of the money from that minimum wage job will you be able to save for your education if you want to escape your parents?

Attend a Tuition-Free School

There are a handful of colleges that don't any cost money to attend if you have one of the following qualities:

○ You are financially needy.

○ You want to work in the college's field of specialty.

○ You are willing to work 15–20 hours a week for the school.

○ You are very smart.

The difficulty with these schools is that the competition for admission can be fierce. Dartmouth College, for instance, is one of many institutions that choose their student body based on merit alone, with no knowledge of each applicant's financial situation. If a low-income person is admitted, the school will (currently) cover that student's entire tuition. However, Dartmouth's combination of Ivy League status, plus reputation as a party school makes it a popular choice for many hopeful applicants, and acceptance is limited to only the exceptional. The highly-acclaimed Deep Springs College considers a person's willingness to milk a cow of greater importance than a strong academic background, so it invites young men with low SAT scores to come on in and apply. Unfortunately, the college only accepts 15 or fewer new students each school year.

University of the People is an up-and-coming educational option for the poverty-stricken. This tuition-free online school is "devoted to providing universal access to higher education." At this time, all the University of the People can offer is knowledge—not an actual degree—but keep checking back, as the school is working toward accreditation.

Take Out a Loan

Everybody knows that they can finance their college education with a student loan, but who wants to sink so far into debt? Here are two methods of borrowing money that won't hit you quite as hard:

1. Loans offered through your financial aid package will be low-interest or subsidized interest. You don't pay any until you've graduated and (presumably) have a job. There are also a number of repayment schedules to choose from.

2. Generous loan forgiveness is available to through many post-graduation programs. Look into the Peace Corps, Teach for America, National Health Service Corps, Equal Justice Works, and many more.

Take Advantage of Internships and Work-Study

Of course, you can always work your way through college little by little. Like your grandfather always says, there's nothing that you can't accomplish with "a strong back and a good work ethic." Put that nose to the grindstone, and make Grandpa proud! But if you want to earn money a little less the old-fashioned way, try one of these ideas:

1. Financial aid saves the day again by offering qualified students a Federal work-study option to help them pay tuition. These jobs can be better than those that people find on their own, because they are often located conveniently on campus and hours are flexible to work with your class schedule. Attempts are also made to find students jobs that will give them experience in their field of study.

2. Speaking of experience in one's field of study, internships are designed to offer just that. Many of these jobs are volunteer positions, but if you can find one that pays a salary or wage, you can glean valuable knowledge and business contacts, while stocking money away for that next quarter of college.

3. If all else fails, become a stripper. You can work evenings, and use your hefty tips to pay for classes during the day.

Fundraise for Your Education

A bake sale probably won't work, because the Girl Scouts already have a monopoly going on neighborhood cookie distribution, but there are all sorts of crazy schemes you can devise to solicit money. Be creative, but keep it safe and legal!

One easy way to get your loved ones to chip in on your education is to set up a simple website where they can enter their credit card information to donate to your cause, anytime and from anywhere. Send out e-mail reminders just before your birthday, Christmas, or any other time when people like to give you stuff. Ask for tuition help instead of traditional gifts.

Win the Lottery

It's a long shot, but it's worth a try, right? There are plenty of chances out there to become instantly wealthy with just a bit of luck and a good psychic to suggest a series of Lotto numbers. If you don't want to invest the dollar to play, be on the lookout for FREE money-offering sweepstakes. Okay, this is the worst advice I've given you yet (except for the stripper thing), but I figure you've gotten bored and stopped reading by now.

10 Tips for Stretching Your College Dollars

Whether you're working your way through school, or paying for everything with scholarship award money, you'll want to make every dollar count. College tuition is expensive, any way you look at it, but there are tricks to getting more bang for your buck in the world of higher education. Here are ten ideas you can consider for getting the most success out of what little you have:

1. **Learn general money management skills.** Instead of just spending until your money is gone, do a bit of budgeting and limit your spending in non-essential areas. Prioritizing your needs will help you appreciate the occasional splurge or treat even more than before! Be aware of student discounts on travel, entertainment, computer software/hardware, any and everything else. Don't forget to keep your student ID handy at all times.

2. **Don't let Wall Street take advantage of you.** Make sure you are getting the best deal available on little financial things like banking fees, credit card APRs, and insurance payments.

3. **Understand tax credits.** Allowable amounts may change from year to year, but make sure to research the possibility of an income tax rebate for college tuition. The IRS won't give it to you without being prompted.

4. **Apply advance placement credits.** Jump on any opportunity that you have to earn cheap or free college credits while you're still in high school. Keep the necessary information on hand so those valuable credits can be applied toward your college degree.

5. **Take more courses at a time.** The price of your college credits often decreases the more you take at a time. You can save money by taking on a heavy class load, as long as you can manage it without making sacrifices in the quality of your learning.

6. **Transfer from a cheaper college to the institution of your choice.** I know you will lose credibility if the medical degree hanging on your wall comes from Ethyl's Backyard University, but it can be a very economical strategy to earn your general education credits someplace inexpensive while you apply for scholarships (or earn money) to attend your dream school. Consider staying close to home so you will qualify for lower tuition at a state-run school, or re-locating to an area with a lower cost of living and more affordable education options. Just check ahead of time to make sure your credits can be transferred to the prestigious school where you'll be earning your bachelor's degree.

7. **Buy used textbooks, and then sell them.** You will not even believe how much a college thinks is an appropriate amount to charge for a stupid BOOK! To make things worse, class instructors will often expect you to purchase two or more different books just to earn three measly college credits! Once you receive your list of textbook requirements for the term, begin searching for cheaper copies from online sellers, or use one of the many "exchange" services like ScrewTheBookstores.com. When you finish a course, unless you loved the subject so much that you want to keep your $130 book to read again later, go back online to sell or exchange your textbooks. As a last resort, your college bookstore probably sells overpriced used books and will also buy them back for around 25 percent of what you originally paid.

8. **Get a roommate...or three.** Living at home with Mom and Dad is usually your least expensive option, but if you're tired of hearing, "Are you really going out dressed like that?" and "Get your filthy feet off the couch, young man," then you might want to find your own place. If your college scholarships don't cover dorm fees, find a few (reliable) friends to share rent and expenses like cable and Internet service. The more people you can pack into one apartment, the less each of you will have to cough up each month. Granted, your roommates will come with their own little annoying habits, but I can almost guarantee that you'll never hear, "Who left this light on?" followed ten minutes later by, "Turn on a light if you're going to read that book in here. Do you want to ruin your eyes?"

9. **Use public transportation.** There's only one thing more expensive than maintaining a vehicle, and that's maintaining a child. The one advantage to money-sucking kids is that they are virtually free to obtain (unless you count the cost of the alcohol that caused you to lose your senses in the first place). You will have to buy your car, and possibly continue to make payments on it for many years to come. Oh, another good thing about kids is that one of yours could grow up to be a professional athlete or famous rock star and make you instantly rich. Your car won't ever give you any of your money back, unless you use it to deliver pizzas. Walk to classes, ride a bike, or take the bus, if you want to see extra funds in your bank account. You say you can't sacrifice the freedom to drive to the beach on weekends? Okay, make friends with someone who owns and maintains a car.

10. **Enroll in college-sponsored healthcare plan.** If you are no longer covered under your parents' health insurance, check to see if your school offers an opportunity for medical coverage before investing in an expensive individual plan. There may be restrictions about which doctors you can see, but for basic medical needs, your premiums will be lower on your college's group plan.

The End is Here!!!!!

Congratulations on finishing my book! Now you have NO EXCUSE not to go out there and win yourself a load of money to help pay your college tuition. I hope I've convinced you that you don't need to be super-smart or mega-talented to succeed in the scholarship game. All it takes is dedication, determination, organization, and any other "-ation" word that I mentioned in the previous chapters and have since forgotten. I know you're ready to get out there and conquer a stack of scholarship applications, but I can't let you leave without spouting the obligatory line you'll hear from every writer of any type of self-help manual:

I DID IT AND SO CAN YOU!!!

Index of Web Resources

The following information was up-to-date as of this book's publication, but is subject to change without notice!

CollegeScholarships.org

Must register to use website? – No

Description: College Scholarships is an awesome website that allows you to browse through specific and non-traditional categories of available scholarships. No need to complete a complicated profile. If you are a twin, click on the "Twins" link; if your parents are broke, click "Low-Income." You can also search by state, career of interest, etc.

Bonus Features: College Scholarships also allows you to browse an extensive list of grants opportunities and student loans. The site's list of resource articles cover interesting topics such as tuition reimbursement and how to write thank you letters to the organizations that have granted you scholarships.

Sweepstakes Offer: No free sweepstakes, but College Scholarships sponsors its own collection of competitive scholarships, including unique opportunities for people who blog or tweet.

TheCollegeAnswer.com

Must register to use website? – Yes

Description: The College Answer is a subdivision of the Sallie Mae (Student Loan Marketing Association) website. After registering, you complete a fun profile about yourself that allows you to make multiple selections in a variety of categories. With any luck, your favorite hobbies, clubs, etc. will be represented in their drop down menus. After you submit your profile, you are matched up with a list of scholarships appropriate to your talents and interests. The results are assigned a percentage number on a scale of how applicable the offer is to your personal profile. You can adjust the "Match Accuracy" bar higher to see only the listings best suited to you, or lower to view scholarships that you may be ineligible to win. You can update your results list at any time by clicking the "Re-run Match" button in the side panel.

Bonus Features: The College Answer provides a complete guide to planning your higher education. You will find educational articles under the headings of Preparing, Selecting, Applying, Paying, Deciding, and Financing.

Sweepstakes Offer: By registering with The College Answer you are automatically entered into a sweepstakes for $1,000. One prize is awarded each month.

Parents are eligible to enter an annual drawing for a $10,000 scholarship if they sign up to receive the Parent Answer e-Newsletter. One prize is awarded per year.

Scholarships4Students.com

Must register to use website? – No

Description: Scholarships4Students is a no-gimmicks website that gives you exactly what you are seeking—plenty of scholarships. The offerings are presented by a series of top category links (example: Heritage Scholarships), followed by sub-category links (example: Armenian, Chicano, Chickasaw, etc.). The top level listings are always available in left menu on each page, which makes for easy navigation from one category to the next.

Bonus Features: Scholarships4Students is a fairly simplistic site, but there are several links at the bottom of the menu that provide resources for homeschoolers, grants, college humor, etc. In case you're in the market for some torturous hazing, the site also offers a directory of existing fraternities and sororities.

Downside: None, unless you hate simplistic websites and prefer to jump through hoops to find your scholarships.

Sweepstakes Offer: None

Scholarships.com

Must register to use website? – Yes

Description: At scholarships.com you will be asked to register, and then complete a fast, but thorough profile for yourself. The system will match you to potential scholarships based on the boxes you click under a series of categories. Your personalized database appears with the scholarships that expire the soonest listed at the top (just beneath the sponsored links), and then proceeds downward to the ones with later deadlines. Click on the scholarship title to learn more details and be directed to the sponsor's website.

Bonus Features: Extras on the website include financial aid information, a college search tool, and a variety of articles teaching study skills and explaining college life (found under "Resources" tab). If this book didn't provide you with enough inspiring examples of real-life scholarship winners to keep you drooling with envy, be sure to check out the website's collection of success stories!

Downsides: Endless pop-up advertisements. If you don't want your email account filled up with offers, you must opt out of four different e-mail lists EVERY TIME that you log into the site.

You cannot view a list of all open scholarships; only those that the system decides you qualify for.

Sweepstakes Offer: The "Tell A Friend" $1,000 Sweepstakes. Refer a friend to sign up for the website, and both of you will receive one entry for a chance to win $1,000 toward college tuition. Odds of winning are slim, as only $1,000 is awarded in a three-month period.

FastWeb.com

Must register to use website? – Yes

Description: FastWeb starts out slow as you create your initial profile. You are asked very few questions about yourself; however, they want to know both your intended college major AND your future career choices, which are essentially the same thing!

After you receive your first list of available scholarships, you are invited to complete your profile with further information about yourself, which is almost guaranteed to result in more scholarship hits. Your category options are sparse compared to other websites, but FastWeb still delivers an extensive list of valuable scholarship opportunities, more, in fact, than most of the similar Internet sites.

One unique and useful feature of the FastWeb scholarship search results page is how they mark along the side of each entry whether the listing is a traditional scholarship, a contest, a promotion, a grant, or some other type of funding offer.

Bonus Features: In addition to scholarship listings, FastWeb provides articles on financial aid, internships, student life, and other topics. The site maintains an active discussion forum where you can ask questions, share stories, and connect with other college hopefuls.

FastWeb will send a TON of e-mails to the account you used when registering. This can be either a bonus or an annoyance, depending on how valuable you find their information.

Downsides: Many special offers to decline.

Poor profile options – FastWeb asks nothing about your additional talents/hobbies, aside from clubs, music, theatre, etc. There is no section to record disabilities or religious affiliation, and your choices are limited in other areas. FastWeb gives you less than ten different races to choose from, and if your parent's career begins with the letter "A," but is not "Air Traffic Controller," then you are out of luck!

Your profile will be displayed as "incomplete" if you are not able to select an option from EVERY category provided. So, if you are not enlisted in the military, if you do not belong to a fraternity/sorority, or if your parents are architects instead of air traffic controllers, you will never know the satisfaction of a completed profile.

You cannot view a list of all open scholarship— only those that the system decides you are qualified to win.

Sweepstakes Offer: FastWeb sponsors contests periodically, but they do not have an ongoing sweepstakes.

ScholarshipExperts.com

Must register to use website? – Yes

Description: Scholarship Experts has the most extensive profile questionnaire on the market, plus a unique method for adding choices from their drop down menus. Carefully read all of the options provided. If you don't click that you have never been charged with a misdemeanor or felony, the system may assume that you have! Once you've received your listing of scholarship possibilities, you'll notice the "Apply Now" button next to each entry. This link will either take you to the website of the scholarship's sponsor, or directly to the actual application. In certain cases, your basic information might be automatically filled in for you.

Bonus Features: Scholarship Experts is all about finding scholarships, but not much else. The site's "E-Organizer" will link you to the government's official site for financial aid information, and also provides a portal where you can search for the perfect college.

Downside: You cannot view a list of all open scholarship, only those that the system decides you are qualified to win.

Sweepstakes Offer: This is not a random sweepstakes drawing, but Scholarship Experts holds an annual "Top Ten List" scholarship competition. They award five $1,000 scholarships each year.

StudentScholarshipSearch.com

Must register to use website? – No

Description: On Student Scholarship Search you do not need to register or sign-in in order to view their scholarship listings (although you have the option to do so). This site seems to have fewer listings than most Internet scholarship searches. I thought I might be granted a more extensive directory if I registered with the website, but nothing changed after my membership was validated.

Bonus Features: Student Scholarship Search is part of the vast family of websites maintained by Student Loan Network. From this site, you can easily navigate to GradLoans.com, FAFSAonline.com, plus other affiliated college-related destinations. Student Scholarship Search also offers a free Scholarship eBook.

Downsides: Every time you click a link on the website, your action opens up a tab for ScholarshipPoints.com. You can avoid this inconvenience by leaving the window open until you are finished browsing "Student Scholarship Search."

At the time of review, some of the site links were outdated and went nowhere.

Sweepstakes Offer: Student Scholarship Search takes sweepstakes to a whole new level with their alternate website ScholarshipPoints.com.

CollegeNET.com

Must register to use website? – Optional

Description: CollegeNET offers an amazing number of scholarship listings. If it's offered, you are likely to find it here! You can search for the perfect scholarship either by entering a keyword or by creating a profile about yourself and requesting matches (if it works—see below). You are able to save the scholarships that interest you to a temporary list for further inspection. The many scholarships offered will appear in order of the highest award amount down to the lowest.

Bonus Features: You can search for and apply to a large number of higher educational institutions right from the CollegeNET website. They also host a very active forum.

Downsides: The profile search is not very accurate. I answered the questions quite specifically, yet found that my fictitious persona was ineligible to receive three out of five of the scholarship results the system produced. For example, my subject was not a resident of Tennessee, his parents did not belong to a union, and he did not have spina bifida, all of which were requirements for the "best fit" scholarships according to CollegeNET.

Once you've created a profile, you must investigate your selected scholarships before closing your browser if you wish to avoid answering the questions again on your next visit. There is no way to save your search results for review on another day.

Sweepstakes Offer: Sign up to participate on the website's forums, then post messages until your fingers bleed! The topics discussed are varied, interesting, and most often do not relate at all to college attendance. The point is to be active and make a lot of friends who will "vote" for you and your cleverly profound forum posts. Every week, someone from the top ten elected members will be chosen to receive a scholarship of anywhere up to $5,000 (the amount varies each week).

CollegeBoard.org

Must register to use website? – Optional

Description: The CollegeBoard.com scholarship search profiler consists of a series of easy-to-use drop-down menus with the categories of "Personal Information," "Academic Information," "Type of Award," and "Affiliation Information." Your search results will show a series of scholarships ranked in alphabetical order, and this list can (optionally) also show federal aid programs, internships, loans, and research grants. When you click to view more information about a scholarship, you will be provided with a very useful description of the award, including detailed eligibility requirements. If you register for the website and log in, you can save your profile and scholarship search results.

Bonus Features: Under their motto of "inspiring minds," CollegeBoard.com offers a wide array of college resource information for students, parents, and even teachers. As a student, you may find "My College QuickStart" to be a useful planning tool. The site also emphasizes preparation for the SAT and other tests, if you're into that kind of thing.

Downsides: The profile questions are far more simplistic than you'll find on other scholarship search websites. For instance, only 14 ethnicities are listed, so if your heritage isn't Arab, Welsh, or one of other 12 offered in between, your ethnic background is deemed irrelevant. This trend continues, with only 10 choices for religious affiliation, five choices of medical conditions, etc.

The profiler never asks you for your GPA or test scores, so the list of scholarship results is likely to include many that you may not qualify for academically.

Sweepstakes Offer: None

MyCollegeOptions.org

Must register to use website? – Yes

Description: The readily visible MyCollegeOptions scholarship listings are limited to the four very basic categories of Location, Major, Ethnicity, and Religion, but with an advanced search, you can add in test scores, a disability, and a keyword. However, after several attempts, I was still unable to complete an advanced search that brought up even a single result! Basically, this is one of the worst scholarship resources out there, but other features of the website make it worth a visit.

Bonus Features: MyCollegeOptions.org offers a great Resource Center containing tons of articles and information for college bound hopefuls. One fun and interesting feature of the site is Zero Hour Threat, a very advanced practice game for taking the ACT and SAT.

There are also areas on the website for parents, counselors, and educators.

Downside: Not so great for finding scholarships.

Sweepstakes Offer: None

CollegeTreasure.com

Must register to use website? – Yes

Description: From the CollegeTreasure.com website: "Our mission is to catalog all of the $11 Billion in college-based merit aid available to make it easy for students to locate schools where they are eligible for scholarships." CollegeTreasure.com catalogs the monetary awards being offered by over 1,200 schools. This website is an excellent resource to check out if you already know which school you plan to attend, or if you want to choose your college based on the number of private scholarships they offer to their students.

Bonus Features: CollegeTreasure.com has a small collection of articles under "College Resources" with some useful titles, such as "Overcoming Test Anxiety" and "Ways to Lower Your EFC" (Expected Family Contribution).

Downside: The website hopes to one day maintain a list of talent-based scholarships, but at this time, you can only search for awards offered directly from each educational establishment. You do not have the option of entering a GPA below 2.7.

Sweepstakes Offer: None

AIE.org

Must register to use website? – No

Description: Adventures In Education (AIE) offers several ways to find scholarships. You can perform a "Quick Search" by entering a keyword or clicking on a category, you can create a profile for an advanced search, or you can simply browse their entire list of scholarships.

Bonus Features: There are many helpful articles on the site, group under the categories of "Planning for College," "Paying for College," "Finding a Career," and "Managing Your Money."

Downsides: Once you've created a profile, you must investigate your selected scholarships before closing your browser if you wish to avoid answering the questions again on your next visit. There is no way to save your search results for review on another day.

If you choose to view ALL of the scholarships offered, you cannot view them in one long list. You must click through the entire database one scholarship at a time.

Sweepstakes Offer: None

Cappex.com

Must register to use website? – Yes

Description: Cappex.com is mainly a college search resource. The website provides tools that will help you to make a list of the institutions of higher learning that interest you the most, connect with them, and track your college applications. Cappex.com provides a planning tool for college visits and a place where you can view "Admission Trends" to see what kind of student is accepted at your schools of choice.

The Cappex.com scholarship search page offers some unique features to help you choose which ones are right for you. In addition to the usual information about amount and deadlines, the website uses a star system to rank the ease of filling out the application and to tell you if the competition for the scholarship is heavy, moderate, average, or "relatively little!" Using a drop-down menu, you can set the "status" of each scholarship on the list with options such as "Might Apply," "Applied," and "Does Not Fit."

Bonus Features: The Cappex Cap Challenge is an opportunity for members to earn achievement awards for participating on the site. The program is described like this: "The idea is simple. The more caps you collect by interacting with colleges, applying to scholarships and navigating the Cappex site, the sooner you can travel through higher levels and gain access to neater stuff. Cappex will guide you along providing hints as to which tasks lead to more caps."

I don't know what they mean by "neater stuff," but earning enough caps will unlock opportunities to apply for certain Cappex-sponsored scholarships.

Cappex.com hosts a number of contests where members can win college money by describing their personal innovations or volunteer service.

Downside: In order to complete your Cappex profile and gain full access to the site features, you must first provide your address and phone number. Some people may not feel comfortable revealing this personal information.

Sweepstakes Offer: Cappex.com doesn't have a sweepstakes lottery, per se, but they offer many of their own scholarships, such as their famous "A GPA Isn't Everything Scholarship," which are said to be awarded based on the extracurricular activities listed in the user's profile. Since the information a member enters on his/her "application" (profile) can't be verified, these scholarships are essentially lotteries.

CollegeProwler.com

Must register to use website? – Yes

Description: CollegeProwler touts itself as having the "The ONLY

College Guides Written By Students for Students." I'm not sure if they actually hold the monopoly on insider college reviews, but the website does have over 200,000 reports from students who ready to share the secret specifics of the institution they attend. You can read reviews about everything from housing to the physical attractiveness of the student population.

As for scholarships, CollegeProwler's search is sorted into the categories of Career Choice, Interests/Hobbies, Major, Military Association, Race/Ethnicity, Religion, Sports, State of Residency. Good descriptions of the scholarships are provided, but some of the listings are out-dated. At least you get a preview of what you can apply for next year!

Bonus Features: CollegeProwler.com runs an online bookstore to provide additional resources, and the site hosts a nice collection of articles about the scholarship application process and other topics relevant to transitioning from high school to college.

Downside: CollegeProwler.com is short on original content. Their scholarship search is powered by SuperCollege.com; visitors are directed to Cappex.com for statistics on college acceptance; connections with colleges are managed through Zinch.com.

Sweepstakes Offer: CollegeProwler holds two monthly lotteries. Their $2,000 "No Essay" Scholarship is open to any prospective college student, and once you are already enrolled in an institution of higher learning, you are eligible to enter their $1,000 Monthly Survey Scholarship by answering a few questions about your school.

FreschInfo.com

Must register to use website? – No

Description: The FreSch! free scholarship search site is another resource for lists of available awards. The profile that they ask you to fill out in order to match you to the right scholarships is short and simplistic. Put in whatever information you want, because it really doesn't matter. I signed up as a Belgian male entering his freshman year of college, and near the top of my search results list I found SIX scholarships in a row that are only awarded to females.

The FreSch! listings may not accurately fit your profile, but one great thing about this site is the feature that allows you to hover your cursor above a scholarship link to read the pertinent details for eligibility. This perk will save you a lot of time and clicks with your back button.

Bonus Features: FreSch! has lots of articles and information about applying for scholarships, getting financial aid, and beyond. Downside: You are only able to see the scholarships that the system matches to your profile answers. Out of the 46 listed on my behalf, the character I created was only eligible to apply for 11 of them. Out of these few, a third of them were simply random lotteries.

In your profile, you are not able to put a decimal point in your GPA. This small detail would be very important if the system actually attempted to match you with only the scholarships that accepted applicants of your academic level.

Sweepstakes Offer: None of their own, but they will link you to everyone else's.

Thank You!

Special thank you to the four people that mean the world to me: my parents William and Elmay Hatcher, my brother Will Hatcher and my husband Derick Pearson, as well as Florence Powell and Louise Hatcher my grandmothers who are my backbone. They may not understand what Facebook and Twitter are but they always made me work hard and continue to serve as daily inspirations.

Special thanks to a few adults who have been inspirational leaders in my life: Marissa Fontaine, who stepped in when my guidance counselor walked out, you helped a bright-eyed slacker get out of high school and jump into college like a Rockstar! Mrs. Konover, Mr. Sicard, Mrs. Smith, Coach Bean and Coach Lisa Johnson, from Atlantic High School, Professor J.A. Welch, Jeff Hatcher, Missey Bailey, James Amps, Nathan Burrell, Lindsay Powell, Sonia Hall, James T, Rev. Crunch and especially Bill Miliken. I owe every step I took in the right direction to them. My mother has always told me to surround myself with positive friends. I thank the following people for answering the phone at 3 a.m. to listen to my new big ideas, and giving me a shoulder to cry on when I fell down: Devin Robinson, Alonie Smith, James Taylor, Jae Arias, Nicole Dure, Chrissy Oberholzer, Kristen Mashburn, Joseph Bostic, Joseph Lowe, Lindia Titus, Tunisha Hubbard, Lola Burford, Brian Buckley, and Sandlie Solomon. Special Thanks to Zeta Phi Beta, Youth Court, Classroom Teachers Association, Florida Residence Access Grant, League of Women Voters and Communities in School for believing in me enough to award me scholarships.

Finally, this book is dedicated to a dear friend Harrington Hall one of the first students that I worked with who was just trying to figure out how to get to college. Your untimely passing has taught me to take chances like there's no tomorrow. You are truly missed!

About the Author

"Look past your circumstances and get creative," is Felecia Hatcher's message when she speaks to crowds around the world. For over a decade, Hatcher has dedicated her life to empowering people around the world to create their own opportunities and live their passion. Hatcher has been honored at the White House for being one of the Empact100's Top 100 Entrepreneurs under 30. Hatcher, who is a TEDx Presenter, has been featured on the Cooking Channel, The NBC Today Show, Inc., in the Wall Street Journal-Japan, Entrepreneur, Essence Magazine and Black Enterprise for her work in Branding, Scholarship Prep and Entrepreneurship.

As a "C" student in high school, Hatcher beat the odds and won over $100,000 in scholarships to attend college by getting creative. Felecia used her experience and knack for personal marketability to start her first business called Urban Excellence as a freshman in college where she built and ran innovative college prep programs for companies like DeVry University, MECA, AMPS Institute, the YMCA, TED center, and the Urban League.

In 2005, Hatcher brushed off her entrepreneurial bug and spent the next few years traveling around the country spearheading successful experiential marketing campaigns for Fortune 500 companies like Nintendo, Sony, Wells Fargo, and Microsoft. Hatcher also worked for the NBA as the Front Office Marketing Manager for the Minnesota Lynx and spearheaded their rebranding campaign.

In 2008, Hatcher started a gourmet popsicle and ice cream catering company after she fell flat on her face while attempting to chase an ice cream truck in heels. The company, which is dedicated to sustainability and innovation, donates a portion of each popsicle sold to charity as well as runs a youth enterprise program called PopPreneurs where Hatcher and her partner teach kids in urban areas how to become entrepreneurs.

Hatcher has formed many strategic partnerships through her company Feverish Ice Cream like Universal Music, Adidas, Whole Foods, Live Nation, Barcardi, JCrew, Capitol Records, Maker's Mark, The U.S. Census Bureau, The W Hotel, Playboy, Tom Cruise, and Vitamin Water to promote their new products through her trucks, carts, social media networks, and sponsored popsicle give-a-ways. Hatcher is the author of two books *The "C" Students Guide to Scholarships* and *How to Start a Business on a Ramen Noodle Budget.*

www.FeleciaHatcher.com

www.CstudentsRock.com

Notes